SEASONAL DANCE

SEASONAL DANCE

How to Celebrate
the Pagan Year

Janice Broch
&
Veronica MacLer

SAMUEL WEISER, INC.

York Beach, Maine

First published in 1993 by
Samuel Weiser, Inc.
Box 612
York Beach, Maine 03910

Library of Congress Cataloging-in-Publication Data
Broch, Janice.
    Seasonal dance: how to celebrate the pagan year / by
Janice Broch and Veronica MacLer.
        p. cm.
    Includes bibliographical references and index.
    1. Witchcraft. 2. Ritual. 3. Religious dance, Modern.
I. MacLer, Veronica. II. Title.
BF1566.B743 1993
299—dc20   93-10003
                                                                CIP

ISBN 0-87728-774-0
CCP

Typeset in 11 point Bembo

Printed in the United States of America

99 98 97 96 95 94 93
10 9 8 7 6 5 4 3 2 1

The paper used in this publication meets the minimum requirements of the
American National Standard for Permanence of Paper for Printed Library Materials
Z39.48-1984.

For Herne, who set my feet on a different path and for Steve, my husband, my lover, and my own personification of the "Lord of the Trees."

Janice Broch

To R. A. J. and H. H. J. — *Ave atque vale.*

Veronic MacLer

We would like to dedicate this book to the memory of Scott Cunningham. We never had the privilege of meeting him, but his kind and generous spirit was revealed in his writing. His great knowledge and his sharing of it will be missed.

Table of Contents

Acknowledgments

First I'd like to thank my Dianic teachers, Eleu and Leuwyn, for providing a warm and caring atmosphere in which to learn my craft. Thanks to Marcelle for moral support and aid far above and beyond the duties of a Maiden and to Lady Phoenix and Larry at Flight of the Phoenix for always having just the right book at their fingertips. Many thanks to all the authors of the songs and chants included, both for creating them and for allowing us to use them. A special thank you to our artist Trish McCall for translating my random images into the beautiful prints she gave birth to. Thanks to our editors at Samuel Weiser who have been both helpful and congenial to work with. For the last minute computer transcription of the music, thanks to Bonnie and her Macintosh and thanks to Michael—he knows what for. And last, but not least, thanks to my husband, Steve, for putting up with computers, ferrets, and my constant shortage of time while this book was being written.

—Janice Broch

Thanks to all those who assisted with the creation of this book: to all the group members for their support, to my husband for his extreme patience and his help in arranging and writing out the music, and to the editors and proofreaders, and to my spirit guides. In addition, I would like to thank Dr. Frederick Turner for his encouragement in my study of ritual and his father, the late Dr. Victor Turner, for providing such a clear path to follow.

—Veronica MacLer

Introduction

The Greenwood Path: Almost twenty years ago, I discovered a small shop in a Dallas suburb. It was a fascinating place full of herbs, delicately scented candles, and colored stones. The shelves were stacked with books, carved wooden candle holders, antiques from England, and crystal balls. If you looked in the dustier, hidden corners, you might find a tiny statue of a god or goddess from long ago or some other treasure that had been overlooked in the tangle of artifacts. The owner of the shop was something called "Wiccan."

I was in college at the time and had been looking for a topic for a series of investigative reporting articles I had to write for a class. The first time I stepped over the threshold of this shop, I knew I had found my subject. I didn't know at the time that I would also find a name for the belief system I had always followed and other people to practice it with. When I found a book in the public library on Wicca and began to read the description of what a Wiccan believed in, it was like feeling a sudden and brisk north wind—I got goose bumps as I saw listed all the things I had believed in since I was a child.

The author of the list was a lady named Doreen Valiente. The book had disappeared from the library when I looked for it again, but I had found Doreen Valiente's name and soon found her excellent books on British Wicca. My contacts at the shop eventually introduced me to a group led by a lady who had been trained by Mark Roberts and Morgan McFarland in the Dianic tradition in Dallas. I attended my first seasonal festival in 1975 and began to study the Dianic path.

This group of people became a second family to me, and for the next thirteen years I would work and practice my craft with them. I went through the Dianic passage rituals and, in 1982, became a High Priestess in that tradition. A combination of events eventually led me to leave that group and form my own, but we continued to celebrate the seasonal festivals together for some time.

During the last few years that I followed the Dianic path, I became increasingly dissatisfied with the practice of eliminating the male element from rituals and celebrations. Once I led my own group, I tried invoking a god as well as a goddess at the beginning of each ritual, but I still had a problem in that the Dianic moon rituals do not use a male element. After an unexpected experience while in Britain, I found Herne, the Hunter aspect of the God, appearing predominantly in my life and spiritual practices. I knew it was time to start some changes, and I began writing balanced seasonal rituals and found the results satisfying.

My new group had been changing things bit by bit, and one day we all looked at each other and unanimously agreed that we couldn't call ourselves "Dianic" anymore. We had grown and evolved, and it was now clear that we were going to have to come up with a new name for what we were doing. All of this led to the decision to form a new tradition that was tailored to fit what we believed and wanted to practice.

Over the next two years, Veronica (then my Maiden, now a High Priestess on her own) and I began work on an expanded and improved set of classes for beginners and a new series of moon rituals and seasonal festivals. Soon everyone was involved, and the results have been rewarding and encouraging. Our group has grown both in size and knowledge, and we feel we are finally finding our path and settling into it. I feel that, although I have been a High Priestess for nearly ten years now, I am finally doing what I went through passage to do.

We have tried to structure our organization so that it is equal in all ways. Priests may preside at moon rituals and festivals as well as priestesses; we celebrate solar and lunar events, and give equal honor and homage to Goddess and God alike. What we basically have tried to create is a tradition that gives equal status and importance to men and women, priest and priestess, God and Goddess. We also felt that we wanted to reclaim the folk ways and more shamanistic practices associated with our craft and eliminate a lot of the "Ceremonial" practices that became popular during the 1950s.

After much thought, we finally settled on *The Greenwood Path* as the name for our new tradition. So far, everyone in our group comes from northern European ancestry, so we have made this our cultural base, with special emphasis on Celtic and British folk ways, which form the basis of modern Wicca. The Greenwood for us conjured up images of ancient forests and living with Nature. The Path is the way to spiritual growth. Together they stand for spiritual attainment and learning through the study of Nature and the following of the Old Ways.

—Janice Broch

• • •

Bridging the Gap: When Janice and I sat down to outline the new classes for beginners, we asked ourselves, "What information did we wish we had been given earlier?" In other words, what did we know now that we wish we had known then?

Before I met Janice, a small group of friends and I were exploring Wicca on our own, with no background whatsoever. We desperately wanted to have a festival for Beltane, but none of us knew what to do. Although we had found a few books that had Beltane rituals in them, none of them were what we had been looking for, and none of them told us how we might do our own.

Some time after I joined Janice's group, it came around to my turn to write a moon ritual. I was terrified. I had attended lots of rituals, sure, and I had a vague idea what they were supposed to sound like, but I had no idea of the meaning, purpose, or staging of a ritual. I was certain I was going to screw it up.

Well, I stumbled through okay, mostly because of my experience as a poet and writer. Over the next few years, I began to study rituals more closely and fell in love with the writing and staging of rituals to the point where I even did a complete series of seasonal rituals as a project for a humanities course in graduate school.

So when Janice and I started to ask what we wished we had been taught, *how to do rituals* was on the top of my list; after all, everyone who joined our group would eventually be expected to write their own rituals, and staging a successful ritual is a wonderful experience that everyone should have at least once. Janice shocked me when she told me that she had been taught even *less* about how to do rituals than I had. A quick survey of our group revealed that everyone else also had the same question: How do you do a ritual, anyway?

We began to work on a study of ritual for our beginning group and tried to come up with a reading list that would help our newcomers understand and create rituals. We found many books on the nature and purpose of ritual, most of them anthropological studies of aboriginal societies. We found lots of books—some good, some not so good—on the meaning and customs associated with the seasonal holidays. We found a few books that were collections of seasonal rituals. However, there was *not a single book* that told how to write and stage Wiccan rituals, or even seasonal rituals in general. We were lamenting this fact to one of our group members when he told us to write one ourselves.

We sat down and began to combine Janice's great experience with seasonal rituals, our years of research into the nature of ritual and the significance of the seasonal holidays, and my experience teaching writing and composition at a local college. This book is the result. It is designed to help you understand the nature and purpose of ritual, why ritual is important in our lives, and what makes a ritual. It gives some suggestions on how to adapt rituals from other sources, how to write rituals of your own, and how to stage them. We have compiled the most complete and up-to-date research that we could find concerning the history and significance of the seasonal holidays. We also offer some of our own rituals as examples, explaining in detail exactly how we staged them, and giving suggestions and ideas for variations and adaptations so that you may take our rituals and make them your own.

As I stated earlier, staging a ritual is something that everyone should experience—nothing can compare to the feeling of having a participant come to you after the ritual, moved close to tears, and say, "That was beautiful. This is what I've been looking for." We wish you many beautiful rituals, and may this book help you find what you are looking for.

—Veronica MacLer

SEASONAL DANCE

Chapter 1

Creating Ritual

> A ritual [is] a rite, a ceremony, a series of symbolic acts focused towards fulfilling a particular intention.
> —Renee Beck and Sydney Barbara Metrick*

A ritual is a way of putting things into an intelligible pattern, a symbolic act that we use to give form to our experience. Rituals help us understand what happens in our lives; they allow us to pass through important changes and transitions by encouraging us to recognize and accept the emotions and fears associated with those changes; they bring us into contact with the past, focus our attention on the present, let us anticipate the future, and connect us with the eternal.

In the past, our ancestors had rituals surrounding every aspect of life: birth, adolescence, marriage, death, and countless others. They also celebrated the life of nature with rituals: every month and season had a holiday with its own significance, purpose, and rites. These rituals were such an integral part of life that they survived long after their original significance was lost, long after science, religion, and philosophy declared them to be mere silly superstition.

---

*Renee Beck and Sydney Barbara Metrick, *The Art of Ritual* (Berkeley, CA: Celestial Arts, 1990), p. 5.

As we entered the 20th century, most people were doing away with rituals as an embarrassing relic of ignorant times. Today, the marriage ritual is often neglected in favor of the simplicity of merely signing a license; "rituals" surrounding the birth of a child are imposed by the medical profession out of physical necessity; teenagers flounder through adolescence, uncertain where childhood ends and adulthood begins. The only holiday that has retained any widespread significance is Christmas, and we often wonder whether it has any meaning other than gift-giving.

Even as many people were phasing out "old-fashioned, outdated" rituals, psychologists were discovering that rituals are vital for us to celebrate, understand, and accept changes in our lives. Certain branches of psychology encourage patients to ritualize particular experiences: trauma, transitions, neglected or repressed emotions, even dreams.[1] Lack of ritual can result in spiritual disillusionment, low self-esteem, and depression.[2] Victims of "the Christmas blues" often have no meaningful ritual associated with this time of year.

A ritual has three basic purposes: 1) to structure experience in a meaningful form; 2) to give expression to unconscious feelings and impulses; and 3) to connect us with the eternal. The first and most obvious reason for ritual is to give meaning to events in our lives. Parties are actually the simplest form of ritual: we celebrate our accomplishments and transitions with family and friends, and this gives them meaning for us.

The second purpose of ritual is to allow us to express feelings and impulses that might otherwise be ignored. The power of ritual lies in its ability to speak to the unconscious, to reach the participants on a subtle level. Because of this, participants often have difficulty vocalizing their reactions to ritual, but the reaction is often much more meaningful than one that can be expressed.

The third and most important purpose of ritual is to form a link between this world and the eternal, archetypal world. Anthropologists

---

[1] From *Festivals*, Feb. 1988; this is a common technique among phenomenologists.
[2] Renee Beck and Barbara Metrick, *The Art of Ritual* (Berkeley, CA: Celestial Arts, 1990), p. 9.

agree that this is the primary function of ritual in archaic or "primitive" cultures—to show that actions are repetitions of things that were done by the gods or ancestors, thereby reminding the people that they are continuing a pattern of action unbroken since the beginning of time.[3] This connection with the eternal is expressed in Wiccan rituals by inviting the gods and spirits to join the participants in the ritual, by making the circle a place that stands "between the worlds"[4]—that is, a bridge between the everyday world and the world of the spirit.

Why Seasonal Rituals?

Once we recognize the need for ritual in our lives, we may still wonder about the numerous seasonal rituals and holidays that our ancestors celebrated. The need for such rituals in an agricultural society is clear. Our ancestors used these rites to mark the important phases of the year—planting, growth, harvest, winter. What relevance can these agricultural rituals have in our modern, urban world?

Simply because we are no longer in daily contact with the changes of the season does not mean that we are no longer affected by them. Our entire ecosystem is tied to the changes of the seasons; as part of that ecosystem, we are tied to them as well. Recent research has suggested that humans are more susceptible to the changes of the seasons than previously thought. Spring fever, the summer doldrums, and the winter blues may be related to such conditions as Seasonal Affective Disorder, in which the lack of strong sunlight in the winter can result in depression and stress-related illnesses. And now, when we are becoming more aware of the interrelatedness and importance of nature, seasonal rituals celebrating the cycle of nature can help us and our children better understand and appreciate the processes of the natural world.

---

[3]Mircea Eliade, *Cosmos and History* (New York: Harper Torch Books, 1959). An excellent summary of the ideas in this book appears in *Parabola*, Summer, 1988.
[4]This is a commonly used phrase in Wiccan groups; the first place we saw it written was in Starhawk's *The Spiral Dance* (San Francisco: HarperCollins, 1989), but we don't know if that is the original source.

For centuries, human beings have tried to understand the meaning of life and death by finding some sort of symbol or metaphor. The one metaphor that we have turned to again and again is that of the cycle of seasons. Seasonal metaphors are extremely powerful; they can be deep and penetrating, and yet they are accessible to everyone. Seasonal metaphors are often used to explain the nature of growing up, growing old, birth, and death to children. Our entire culture—poetry, music, history, drama, religion, literature—is centered around seasonal myths.

Seasonal rituals, with their accompanying metaphors, can fill the gaps in our ritual lives, including helping us make the major transitions, as well as the hundreds of "little" transitions—ones we may not even realize are worthy of acknowledgment. Seasonal metaphors can be used to structure any aspect of our lives; any experience can be understood by the cycle of birth, growth, death, and rebirth.

Perhaps this is the primary advantage of seasonal rituals—that they celebrate all aspects of life. No experience is devalued or seen as completely negative; the end of one thing is merely clearing the way for something new. Seasonal rituals see beauty in winter as well as spring; they teach us the necessity and value of death and decay as well as birth and growth.

In our explanations of the seasonal holidays and sample rituals, we have used Wiccan patterns and themes for a number of reasons. The primary reason is that Wicca is based on pre-Christian Celtic and Anglo-Saxon customs and traditions, which form the basis of British and Western European ethnic culture, much of which has now been lost. Also, the eight holidays used by Wiccans are common to many different cultures and are easily adapted to fit any tradition. Veronica's Ostara (Vernal Equinox) ritual, for example, is based on Babylonian, Egyptian, and Greco-Roman myths and traditions.

The four minor holidays—the solar holidays—come from the Germanic, Norse, or Anglo-Saxon tradition. They are the winter and sum-

---

[5]Of the solar holidays, the solstices are far more important, and there is evidence that the celebration of the equinoxes is a late import into Britain. The Norse and Saxons celebrated a spring festival in March and a harvest festival in September, but we know

mer solstices and the spring and autumn equinoxes.[5] The four major holidays—Samhain (October 31), Imbolg (February 2), Beltane (May 1), and Lammas (August 1)—are believed to be originally lunar holidays, and they come from the early Celtic or even pre-Celtic cultures. The four major holidays are also called *cross-quarter days*, because they fall exactly between the solstices and equinoxes and divide each quarter of the year in half.

As different cultures met and combined, people adopted new holidays alongside their old ones, unconcerned with any apparent conflict that might have developed. The Saxons celebrated Samhain with their Celtic cousins, and the Celts picked up the habit of celebrating Yule even though both holidays represented the beginning of the new year, two months apart. We have compiled the most complete explanations of the significance of each holiday that we could, and where possible we have combined the various traditions into a consistent myth of the year.

Please note that these are not the only holidays, but over the world and over the years these have appeared again and again as the most important celebrations; they continue to be recognized even when their original significance has long been lost. These holidays are the basis of many of our modern celebrations and contain themes and ideas that have long been forgotten.

Parts and Pattern of Ritual

Rituals consist of three major parts: the introduction, the ritual action, and the closing. The introduction creates sacred space and states the purpose of the ritual. The ritual action is the "meat" of the ritual, the reason for the coming together. The closing releases the space back into the mundane world. In a Wiccan ritual, each part tends to follow the pattern described below.

---

little specific information about these holidays, not even whether they were actually celebrated on the equinoxes.

INTRODUCTION

This consists of invocations to the elements and the God and/or the Goddess, the creation of sacred space, and a short explanation of the reason for coming together. In a seasonal ritual, this explanation will often be a brief explanation of the holiday. The space of the ritual can be made sacred in a number of ways; there are various rites and ceremonies for a complete casting of a circle. The method we use at holidays is very simple: people naturally fall silent as we enter the circle, walking clockwise till we find a place to sit. Then we invoke the spirits, join hands, and declare the space closed and consecrated. Since our group never does any work on holidays, we have always found this sufficient. Use whatever you feel is necessary and appropriate.

An invocation can be a simple invitation to spirits of the elements, or it can be elaborate. Often invocations are short and ad-libbed, though sometimes they may be written up as part of the ritual. Our group always uses a candle at each quarter for each element (north/earth, east/air, south/fire, west/water) and a symbol and herb that represent each element. When the element is invoked, the candle is lit, and the herbs are offered in the cauldron. The invocations need not necessarily come at the opening of the ritual; sometimes you may choose to wait until the middle of the ritual before invoking the elements either for convenience or for dramatic effect. Invocations to the God and Goddess are usually more formal and are more often written especially for the ritual. Our group has certain patterns of invocations that we like to use over and over. Again, we always light a candle for the God and one for the Goddess as they are invoked.

RITUAL ACTION

Also called the drama or performance, this is the point of the ritual, the center of focus, the manifestation of the myth. The ritual action will often involve some kind of lesson, the repetition of a myth, for example; some type of "working" that asks for the power of the season to be present in our lives or for help in understanding the lesson of the season; and some way of internalizing the ritual experience for each individual involved. This internalization can be giving each person a symbol of the ritual or merely passing a symbol around to let each person meditate on it and derive his or her own significance from it.

CLOSING

In a Wiccan ritual, the closing usually has two parts: communion and thanksgiving. Communion reinforces the connection among the group and the group's connection with the unseen; the simplest form of communion is the passing of the chalice. In thanksgiving, the group thanks the elements, the God and/or the Goddess for their presence and participation, then opens the circle. Thanksgiving is usually very informal: the same person who invoked each element usually says a few simple words of thanks, sometimes even done silently, and blows out the candle. The priest or priestess who invoked the God and Goddess thanks them for their presence and blows out the appropriate candle; this is usually slightly more formal, often written into the ritual. Then the priest or priestess declares the circle open.

AFTER THE RITUAL

In our group, we always have a potluck dinner or snacks after the ritual. This is an excellent chance for the group to socialize and reinforce the connections that brought it together in the first place. This also serves to let the force of the ritual "sink in" while you are still among the people who participated. It is also a great chance for a party. Remember—this is a holiday, so celebrate!

Building a Ritual

Since ancient times, rituals have tended to have two major parts. The mysteries at Eleusis were divided into "the things said" and "the things done." The Catholic Mass is divided into the "Liturgy of the Word" (things said) and the "Liturgy of the Eucharist" (things done). For our purposes, we will borrow some terms from modern theater: *text* and *staging*. Think of the text as *what you would like to say* and the staging as *how you say it*.

Rituals can vary in the amount of text and the amount of staging, depending on the purpose of the ritual, the audience for whom it is intended, and the whim of the person doing the ritual. There are meditative rituals that are completely text with no action, and mute rituals that consist solely of pantomime with no explanatory text. Most rituals fall somewhere in between. A balance between text and action is usually most effective; straight monologue can cause the audience to feel bored or left out, and straight pantomime may leave the audience wondering what's going on. A ritual need not be a complicated theatrical production; the text may simply be the explanation of the holiday or the repetition of a myth, and the staging may consist of dividing the text among two or more voices in a choral reading.

When building a ritual, you may find a text that appeals to you and then figure out something to do with it. You might also think of something you would like to do and then construct a text around it. In other words, there are a number of ways to gather the text of your ritual and decide how to stage it.

Adapting the Text

Don't be afraid to use a ritual printed in a book somewhere. The person who wrote the ritual didn't publish it so it would stay lifeless on the page. If one of our rituals strikes you, *please use it!* The only rule that applies when you use someone else's material is to cite it. This doesn't mean that you interrupt your ritual to give a footnote; you can mention your source before you start, but only if it will not break the mood. If anyone asks you about the ritual, tell him or her where you got it. The person may want to see what else that author has written for use in a future ritual. Also, if you found a ritual in a book, there's a good chance that someone in your group has also found it or will at some time; citing your source up front will save you some embarrassment later. No one will fault you for using someone else's material, but they will fault you for claiming it as your own.

Not every group is the same; something that worked well for us may be completely inappropriate for your group. That's fine. That's why we've given suggestions for adapting the sample rituals — to give you some ideas of what can be done with them. Feel free to adapt material from any source and change it as you need to. Again, the only rule is, if you adapt something from another source, make a note of it somewhere on the ritual. This is as much for yourself as it is for the author; you know the source now, but in a few years, who knows? And if you pass the ritual on to anyone else, he or she may want to know as well. There is one favorite piece that our group has used for over ten years, and we know it was originally adapted from another source. However, the person who adapted it did not make a note of the source, and we have no way of knowing where it came from, how old it is, what the original sounded like, or if there is any more to it. Trust us, it is maddening!

While we're talking about adapting things, let us give you a hint. Look at old, traditional, folk material — poems, songs, charms, legends. These can add a great touch to a ritual, even if they are just tacked on in the opening. Don't forget your favorite poets, singers, and writers when you are looking for material for a ritual. We have done rituals based on Chaucer, Shakespeare, W. B. Yeats, Rudyard Kipling, Ben Jonson, and Robert Burns, as well as many inspired by old folk songs or legends. Modern songs are fine, too, though it may be harder to find modern songs that fit your theme.

Writing the Text

Suppose you want to write a ritual, or at least the major part of one, completely from scratch. Writing and performing your own rituals is by far the most satisfying experience of all, and it will often mean that much more to your group. But how do you go about it?

The only rule involved in writing a ritual is this: *allow yourself at least four weeks, even six or eight.* The last thing you want to do is force a ritual; give yourself plenty of time to meditate about your ritual, to throw away ideas, and start all over again. Also, when writing a ritual, you will find yourself fussing over minute turns of phrase, wanting it to be absolutely perfect. Then you still have to worry about decorations, staging, music, and hundreds of other things. And you never know what may come up between now and then. In our group, we assign smaller, monthly rituals at least a month or two in advance, and the larger, seasonal rituals are all assigned at the beginning of each new year.

When you sit down to write your ritual, there are certain steps you can follow to help you. These steps are based on the "Writing Process," the current method of teaching composition and creative writing in colleges and universities, with special adaptations for seasonal rituals. All writers go through a similar process, whether they realize it or not. Many writers find that understanding this process will help them get through the rough parts and overcome writer's block, whether they follow the steps consciously or not. The following steps are designed to help you, especially if you get stuck, not to stifle your creativity. If you find yourself inspired and can turn out a complete, finished ritual in one sitting, great! If not, try working through these steps. (Although these examples pertain to seasonal rituals, the same steps apply to any ritual.)

RESEARCH

Before you can talk about anything, you have to know what it is you're going to talk about. The first step in writing a ritual is to learn about your topic or subject. If, for instance, you are going to write a Beltane ritual and you have never even heard of Beltane before, you're going to have a lot of trouble coming up with ideas. If you already know a little bit about Beltane, then you're one step ahead.

Another reason to research is to get an idea of what people have done on this holiday in the past—customs, traditions, and legends make excellent rituals. We've done a Samhain (Halloween) ritual based on carving a Jack O'Lantern, using the origins and folktales of the Jack O'Lantern as our text.

Research can be anything from looking up a word in a dictionary to doing a doctoral dissertation. So how do you know when you've done enough? When you think you have at least maybe a rough idea of what you might possibly do, then you've done enough. Don't be frightened by the vast number of sources available, and don't think that you have to read *everything*. The purpose of research is to give you something to think about, something about your subject that you can relate to. When you feel like you have a place to start, then start! The books will still be there later—your ideas might not be.

EXPERIENCE

A ritual is most effective when the experience of the ritual carries over into everyday life. The best (and easiest) way to make a ritual experience work for everyone is to start with your own experiences. Is there anything about this holiday/season/time of year that has a special meaning for you? What do you think of when you think of this season? Did you find anything in your research that related to your own life? If you can't think of anything, ask a friend. Experience is an excellent way to get meaningful ideas and images, even if research gets you nowhere.

> When I set out to write my first Autumn Equinox ritual, I found very little information available, and what I found was conflicting. So I sat down and thought about that time of year and what I associated with it. I grew up in Arizona, where early fall means monsoon season: a time of sudden, violent thunderstorms after a scorching summer. That was a powerful image for me, so I started with that idea and related it to the idea of the equinox as a time of rebalancing.
>
> — Veronica

BRAINSTORMING

Think about your subject. Make a note of anything and everything that comes to mind. Don't try to sift through what you like and don't like, and don't judge the ideas that come to you; all that will do is interrupt your train of thought. After you have written down everything you can think of, go back through and decide what you like or don't like. Often, you can get a good list of ideas to work with from one brainstorming session; if you're lucky enough to be inspired, one brainstorming session can give you the major part of your ritual. If your first brainstorming session draws a blank, set it aside. Go do something else and come back to it later. Basically, what you want to do is let the ideas you have "sink in." There are a number of ways of doing this; the trick is to find out which ones work for you.

1) *Meditation* — sit or lie comfortably in a quiet place. Turn the lights out and light a candle if you want; you can also play some soft music. Just think about your subject, what you know about it, any experiences you have, and let your mind have a chance to play with the ideas. The trick to making this work is not to force anything; don't get frustrated if nothing seems to come right away.

2) *Put it on a "back burner"* — all you do is go about your normal routine, and when you find your mind starting to wander, let it wander back to your ritual. You'll be amazed how much time there is during the day when our bodies are occupied but our minds are free: cooking, cleaning, riding a bus, driving a car, that grey area between sleeping and waking. (Veronica claims she does her best thinking in the shower or bathtub.) The biggest trick to this technique is to always have something to jot down notes on. There is nothing more frustrating than coming up with the perfect phrase or image and then forgetting it before you get a chance to write it down.

3) *Invocation* — charge a candle for the ritual you are working on and burn it over a few days, asking whatever god and/or goddess you'd like to use in the ritual and any other appropriate spirits for help and inspiration. (Janice swears by this method, saying that she will receive good ideas in her dreams when she does this.)

If you still can't come up with any idea whatsoever, you might want to do a little more research. Ask another friend. Read one more chapter in a book. After each new input, try another brainstorming session.

THEME

Now that you have some ideas about your subject, the next thing you need is a theme. Many people confuse the subject and the theme, and they find themselves having trouble because of it. The distinction is very simple: the *subject* is the thing that you are talking about, and the *theme* is what you are saying about it.

The theme doesn't have to be a concrete statement. It could be a feeling, an image, a memory. What is the purpose of this ritual? What do I want it to do? What message am I trying to convey? What feelings and experiences do I want people to come away with? The answer to all of these questions is the theme.

STRUCTURE (OUTLINE)

Once you have a theme, once you know what you want to say, the next step is to decide how to say it. A ritual can be song, dance, drama, storytelling, poetry, prose, any combination of these, and anything else that strikes you. Structure at this point consists of a vague idea or loose outline of what you might like to do, taking into consideration your audience and available resources. Don't be surprised if you find yourself changing the structure as you progress; you may want to add, drop, or change entire sections as you find new material and come up with new ideas.

CONTROLLING IMAGE OR IDEA

This is poets' jargon for "what ties everything together." The controlling image is a continuing metaphor used throughout the ritual that brings the text and staging into a unified whole. It can be a symbol, an event, an idea, a myth—anything. It can be an obvious part of the ritual, or just something you can keep in the back of your mind as you build your ritual. The controlling image is the base on which your ritual stands; it will influence your entire ritual, from decorations to performance. It is a guide and a fence, giving you both a direction and a limit when you are gathering ideas.

GATHERING IDEAS

Here is where it all comes together. Keeping your theme and controlling image in mind, take your brainstorming lists and pick out those ideas, images, symbols, words, and phrases that you like the best—that mean the most to you. Use your structure as a skeleton and start piecing the ideas together around it. Then connect your ideas, and you have a ritual.

To give you a better idea of how this works, let's walk through the steps using Veronica's Lammas ritual on page 99.

Veronica: I knew that Lammas was a harvest festival, and also that it was the festival of the Sun God, Lugh. I decided to concentrate on the harvest aspect, and I already had a lot of images in mind. Because Hallowe'en and Thanksgiving are also harvest celebrations, I had everything associated with them to work with: apples, pumpkins, wheat, harvest moon, beginnings of cold weather, leaves turning color, etc.

Now I knew what my subject was, and I had a lot of ideas and symbols. It was time to decide on a theme. What did I want the ritual to say? to do? I wanted to convey the idea of harvest in nature being symbolic of things coming to fruition in our lives, kind of a "personal" harvest. I decided to have everyone help charge a group candle with something they wanted to come to fruition in their personal lives. Then we would light the candle, encouraging our personal fruits to ripen as nature ripened around us. The flame of the candle would stand in for the sun, ripening our personal harvest as the sun ripens the fields. Some kind of chant while we burned the candle seemed perfect, something that would link the ripening fields to the candle we were burning.

Then I got stuck. How could I relate a burning candle to a harvest? I went back over my list of images, looking for a controlling idea. What image or symbol could tie all this together? What do a candle and a ripe field in autumn have in common? Color. A candle flame and a field of ripe wheat are both yellow-gold. I had my controlling idea: the color gold. This gave me the lines:

> Gold, gold the candle burns.
> Gold, gold the wheatfield turns.

The short, rhymed sentences had the rhythmic, chant quality I was looking for, and they were simple and easy to remember, perfect for a chorus.

I went back through my list of images, picking out those that had anything to do with gold. I then collected them into rhymed couplets (sometimes stretching a rhyme or two, but if Shakespeare can do it, so can we) and added a few lines referring to the things coming to fruition in our lives. I then looked back through what I'd written to see if I could put it into some logical order.

The lines about our personal harvest fell into chronological order: intent, action, and results. I grouped the remaining couplets according to element/directional images, arranged them north-east-south-west, and pieced the two together. I had the bulk of my harvest ritual. I then added the introduction and closing, and it was finished.

Staging the Ritual

A ritual can consist of anything from the simple reading of the text to an elaborate theatrical performance with music, dance, and costumes. How much you want to do for your rituals is going to depend on what you think is appropriate for your group, the materials and time you have available, and what you want to do. The rituals we give here as examples show a pretty wide spread of complexity, depending on our audience and what we felt like doing. There is no "right" or "wrong"; listen to your own heart. When it works for you, then it is right.

When you sit down to stage your ritual, you will probably already have a few ideas about staging from the structure of your text, but you may want to formalize the action, maybe dress it up a little. Following is a list of the most common components of a ritual, and some suggestions on how to use them.

POETRY

Poetry has been part of ritual since the beginning of history. Verse, meter, and rhyme transform the message from ordinary and mundane to different and special. It is possible, though somewhat difficult, to do a ritual completely in verse, but just the addition of a poem at the opening of a ritual will greatly enhance it. A balanced combination of poetry and prose is very effective and not very difficult.

MUSIC

The presence of music can add a lot to a ritual, even if it is only a tape playing in the background. We have also done rituals that consist of a single voice singing a meditative song. However, because singing together is an excellent way to raise energy and unite a group, music usually works best if it is a simple song or chant that everyone knows. Our group has a few simple rounds and chants that we use almost every time; everyone learns them very quickly, and the effect of everyone singing together is tremendous. Appendix A contains all the songs we used in the sample rituals, complete with music.

If you plan to have a lot of singing in your ritual and want some background noise that won't compete, try some of the "Sounds of Nature" or "Environment" tapes—a tape of a thunderstorm in the background will add a lot to a ritual centering around a storm.

DANCE

Dance is another ancient, powerful part of ritual. There are two basic types of dances: simple circle dances that the group does together, and dances that are done as a performance by a few members for the others. A performance dance need not be expertly done or even choreographed; spontaneous movement generated by the feelings evoked in the ritual can be very effective. In Appendix B there are a few simple circle dances that you may want to use in your group, with suggestions on how to alter them.

ALTARS

Your altar is the focal point of your ritual. It is usually the center of activity and is the physical center of your circle of participants. The altar is the most visual representation of what you are trying to say with the ritual itself. Needless to say, it should be decorated with care. It will set the tone with its colors, goddess and god statues, and arrangements. It is usually best to really think about your altar and 'design' it ahead of time. You might even want to make a diagram of where you will place what so you can visualize it better. Although careful thought is a good idea, it's also fun to let everyone participate in decorating the circle. Having a "scavenger hunt" for natural objects to use as decorations when doing an outdoor ritual can provide a special touch to the altar.

Most of the seasonal festivals have obvious themes for decorations associated with them. For a harvest ritual the altar could be decorated with fruits, vegetables, and sheaves of wheat or corn dolls. An Imbolg ritual could be very wintery in its decorations. Using a lot of crystals, mirrors, silver candlesticks, a silver or crystal chalice, and many, many candles create a stunning effect of shimmering, icy, winter. Visually, it's more appealing if you stick to colors that blend together and don't mix your styles too much. An altar decorated with oak leaves, pinecones, wood, and rocks is going to make a Waterford crystal goblet look a bit out of place. A wooden or pottery chalice would be more at home in such a setting.

Another thing to consider when decorating your altar is what sort of cultural effect, if any, you are trying to achieve. If you want the circle to have an Egyptian feel to it then do some research into Egyptian temples and see what the art and artifacts looked like. Your deity statues will go a long way in making a cultural statement. Statues from most of the classical cultures are easily found in museum shops or from the numerous companies that are making reproductions precisely to be used in modern Pagan circles and rituals. Several of these are noted in

Figure 1 (top). *A basic Pagan altar set on a flat rock for an outdoor ritual. The knife represents the God or male principle; the chalice represents the Goddess or female principle; the bell signals the beginning of the ritual; and the bowl holds herbs — gifts to the God and Goddess. The horn-like object is a decorative chalice that is sometimes filled with flowers of the season.*

Figure 2 (bottom). *Another way to set up an altar using different types of items and the added decoration. The chalice and knife represent the God and Goddess; the herbs are in a small container; the bell signals participants; and the candelabra and antlers represent the fall season.*

our Resources section as well as a source to obtain representations of harder to find gods or goddesses.

There are certain standard items usually present on a Pagan altar. At least two candles, one normally representing the God and one the Goddess, are the standard, but you can add more if you want to get elaborate. You might want to have one to represent each of the different aspects of the deities you will be using, or you might like a lot of candles for the effect. As you face the altar, the candle on the left represents the Goddess, the one on the right, the God. Another candle, a service candle, sits off to the side. This is passed to the elements so they can light the candles at the directional points and is used by the priest or priestess to light the altar candles.

A chalice representing the Goddess or feminine principle will usually contain wine or water. We've been known to fill ours with Irish Creme, so the contents are up to you. A knife or wand is common as a representation of the God or male principal. A bell is used to signal the beginning of the ritual and to call the participants to enter the circle. A small container holds herbs that are gifts to the God and Goddess. One of the standards we use is patchouli for the God and Life-everlasting for the Goddess with a dash of cinnamon on top. Cinnamon makes pretty "sparkles" of light when put into the cauldron. Although we never do this, some traditions also have elemental representations on the altar. These are the common basics to an altar. The rest of the decorations are set by the theme and your own imagination and budget. (See figures 1 and 2 on page 18 for examples of basic altar setups.)

The altar is, of course, a special place that is your own place of worship. It is a place to honor the season and the attendant deities that you will be evoking. We set up our altars so that the priest and priestess will be facing the north when they are standing at the altar as the north is considered the place of power and mystery. You might want to obtain a small table to be used as an altar. For outdoor rituals an old stump makes an excellent altar, as does a large flat rock. Or the altar can be set up directly on the floor or ground with maybe nothing more than an ornamental cloth under it. After a little experimentation you'll find what suits you and your group the best.

DECORATIONS, PROPS, AND COSTUMES

Decorating a circle is an excellent way of setting it apart from the everyday, and wearing costumes when doing a ritual immediately tells your audience that this is something special. As we discussed earlier, circle decorations usually center around the altar, where everyone can see them. The most common types of decorations are plants and greenery, horns and antlers, crystals, candles, feathers, and some symbols or statues of the God or Goddess used in the ritual. Appendix C contains some basic symbols for each direction and element as well as for the God and Goddess.

Costumes can be elaborate, or they can be very basic symbols designed to remind the audience of what you're trying to evoke. For instance, in one Imbolg ritual where three women portrayed the Triple Goddess, one dressed in white with flowers in her hair to represent the Maiden; another dressed in red carrying a sheaf of wheat to represent the Mother; and a third dressed in black with her face veiled to represent the Crone. In a Beltane ritual, the Priestess simply wore a silver sash to represent the Maiden aspect of the Goddess, and the Priest wore a yellow headband as the Sun King aspect of the God.

The most common props are candles, incense, cakes, and a chalice of juice or wine. When indoors we always use a small cauldron to burn some rubbing alcohol; this represents the bonfires that were traditionally done at all the holidays and are impractical indoors. Props are also used for symbols of the ritual that people may take home with them as a way of internalizing the experience of the ritual. We often use stones, small clay figures, pieces of antler or bone, flowers, seeds, feathers— any small, inexpensive thing that would be a good symbol of the ritual. For each sample ritual, we give a list of the props we used, along with directions on how to make them.

• • •

There are a number of things to consider when staging a ritual. How big a group are you expecting? Is this your audience's first experience with ritual? How can you involve your audience in your ritual? Usually, rituals are more effective if they are interactive—that is, if they invite the audience to participate in the ritual itself. The most common means of doing this are chants, songs, or dances that everyone does together. However, if you have some people who have little or no experience with ritual, they may feel awkward or uncomfortable if they are expected to participate and don't know what to do.

There are a number of ways to solve this problem. First, you can depend on a small number of people who know the songs and chants to help any newcomers and encourage them to join in. This is what our group does most often, and it has always worked. We provide enough slips of paper with the words to the chant for everyone, and there are usually enough "regulars" to help the guests along. Second, if possible, you can take some time before the ritual to teach the group any songs or dances that you may wish to use. The important thing for either of these solutions is to keep it *simple*. If your regulars get confused, everybody will.

The third solution to this problem is to make your ritual more theatrical, so that the audience is comfortable being an observer rather than a participant. This works best for an introductory ritual to a new group with little ritual experience, but it can also provide a change of pace for a regular group. The only problem with doing a completely non-participatory ritual is that your audience might get bored. This is where ritual and theater overlap; costumes, props, and lots of action can keep your audience intrigued without expecting them to participate.

How you stage your rituals will depend on availability, purpose, and audience. If you can't find anything to use as costumes, then do it without them. If you really want this ritual to bring your group together as a united whole, then you will want to make it very interactive. If you want your ritual to teach your group something, then maybe it should be more meditative than theatrical. If this is your audience's first experience with ritual, you probably don't want to make them do element invocations and complicated circle dances.

The sample rituals in the next eight chapters run the gamut from complete audience participation to pure theater; we have given two sample rituals for each of the major holidays and one sample ritual for each of the minor holidays. Before each ritual, we explain the purpose and type of audience the ritual was aimed at. The directions for costumes, decorations, and staging represent the way *we* did it, not the way it *has* to be done. After each ritual, there are ideas for variations you may want to try and hints on how you might adapt these rituals for your own use. Remember, the only "right" way is the way that works for you and your group.

NOTES ON THE SAMPLE RITUALS

In the following rituals, the terms "Priest" and "Priestess" refer respectively to the man and woman who are staging the ritual, usually the person who wrote the ritual and his/her partner. We find it best to have a priest play the part of any gods and a priestess play the part of any goddesses, but it doesn't really matter who says what. In the ritual, the note "Priest/Priestess" indicates that the text may be read by either a priest or a priestess, usually defaulting to whoever is actually responsible for putting on the ritual. The terms "Maiden" and "Squire" simply refer to any woman or man who assists the priest or priestess, either reading secondary parts or assisting with props, chants, songs, and dances. The note "Maiden/Squire" indicates that assistant may be either male or female. We usually try to balance parts between males and females, but availability, emphasis of certain themes, and need for variety sometimes tip the scales.

Element invocations can be read by anyone; our group asks for volunteers, so people can invoke the elements they have an affinity for. This is also a good way to get the willing members of the audience to participate. When we have written invocations, we simply give them to our volunteers on small, unobtrusive slips of paper. If the element invocations are not written, the ritual will just say "Invoke the elements."

Invocations to the God and Goddess are usually done by the Priest or Priestess who is putting on the ritual, or the Priest can invoke the God and the Priestess the Goddess; we tend to avoid this second option because we often have priests who have an affinity for a particular goddess and priestesses who have an affinity for a particular god. In general, whoever volunteered to do the ritual decides who does what.

In the rituals that follow, lines meant to be said by the entire group are indicated in the text. Unless otherwise mentioned, the audience for each of the rituals is our regular group and a small number of guests, usually ten or fifteen people in all.

Chapter 2

Samhain

Samuin	**Hallowe'en**
Nutcrack Night	**Mischief Night**

Originally the Celtic New Year, Samhain[1] is the intercalary day (the "day" of "a year and a day") of the old Celtic calendar. Because of this, Samhain is a day that is not a day, and a time that is not a time, because it is really outside of the year. This is why divination, usually marriage divination using apples and hazelnuts, is so common on this night. Samhain night exists "between the worlds," and the veils that divide the natural from the supernatural world are very thin. This is also the reason that Samhain is the best night to see the fairies—Samhain night is when the Sidhe (*shee*) or fairy mounds open.

In the Ulster cycle of Irish myths, Samhain is the festival during which the king gathered all of the warriors at the great hall of Tlachtagha at Munster and bestowed gifts on them. The king's champion was also named at this festival. The festival itself lasted seven days: the three days preceding Samhain, Samhain itself, and the three days following Samhain. Samhain probably gained its association with death

---

[1]Pronounced *saw-in* or *sow-in* (rhymes with *cow*) in Irish Gaelic (Samuin is the Irish spelling), *sah-veen* in Scots Gaelic, and *sah-vine* or *sah-vin* in Welsh.

Figure 3. Samhain.

from the Celtic practice of slaughtering herds at this festival; this practice had two purposes: first, to store up enough meat for the winter, and second, to cull out any animals that would not survive the harsh winter.[2]

It is on Samhain that the spirits of the dead return to their former homes to bless or curse the current inhabitants. To ensure a blessing, the family would retreat to one side of the house, leaving food, wine, and light on the other side, so the ancestors could make themselves at home. This practice is still followed in parts of the Celtic world today, and this same custom is followed by many Wiccans under the name of the "Dumb (or Mute) Supper." The custom of "souling," nowadays generally associated with Christmas caroling, is actually part of this old Samhain tradition, where masked soulers—thought to represent the spirits of the dead—would go from door to door collecting gifts of food and threatening the most outrageous and amusing punishments to those who did not contribute. This is the origin of our modern-day "trick-or-treating."[3]

Harvest symbols are very common for Samhain—apples especially, but also pumpkins, nuts, wheat, etc.—and are usually found in any altar decorations. However, at Samhain, the harvest is already in, and so the emphasis is shifting from the physical concerns of harvest and growth to the more spiritual side of rest, meditating on death, preparation for the winter, and waiting for the return of spring.

Samhain opens the dark half of the year. This is the first day of winter, the beginning of the season of death. This is the time when the Hunter comes into his own in his aspect of Guardian of the Gates of Death. In some regions, Herne the Hunter begins his Wild Hunt on Samhain night and continues throughout the winter.

Samhain is also ruled by the *Cailleach*, the winter hag.[4] This is the feast of the Crone or Death-Goddess, either in the form of Arianrhod

---

[2]Jeffrey Gantz, *Early Irish Myths and Sagas* (London, England: Penguin Books, 1981), pp. 12–13.
[3]Madeleine Pelner Cosman, *Medieval Holidays and Festivals: A Calendar of Celebrations* (New York: Charles Scribner's Sons, 1981), pp. 82–84.
[4]Caitlin Matthews, *Elements of the Celtic Tradition* (Shaftesbury, England: Element Books, 1989), p. 86.

(*Caer Arianrhod*, the "Castle of Arianrhod," the Welsh name for the Aurora Borealis, was the place to where the spirits of the dead ascended) or of *Cerridwen* (the keeper of the magic Cauldron of Inspiration from which all wisdom comes). The Crone is also the mistress of magic and the keeper of riddles. She will pass on her knowledge only to those who can answer her riddle.

The recognition and celebration of death as a necessary part of regeneration is the message of Samhain. Meditation on the paradox that death is also a birth and that creation requires the destruction of the old can provide the answer to the Crone's riddle.

Samhain Ritual #1
by Janice

Purpose: This ritual celebrates Herne the Hunter moving into his aspect of Guardian of the Gates of Death and the beginning of the Wild Hunt, so it is dedicated to the God as Herne the Hunter. Because of this, the priest plays a major role even though the priestess is actually doing the ritual.

We like to make Samhain a big party; everyone comes in costume, and we always have games and contests before the ritual with simple, inexpensive prizes for the winners (candy, fruit, candles, crystals, etc.). Some games we use are listed in Appendix D.

Decorations: Decorate the circle with harvest symbols: apples, pumpkins, gourds, corn, and nuts. At the altar have a pair of antlers and a knife, sword, or arrow.

Necessary props: A basket filled with moss and tiny, clay deer fetishes[5] nestled in the moss should be placed on the altar. The cauldron should be as large as possible, and the chalice should be dark and earthy-

---

[5]A fetish can be anything that has magical or ritual significance, but the fetishes we refer to are similar to those of Southwestern Indians: carved stone or clay figures that represent an animal spirit. The fetish figure itself acts as a material "housing" for the spirit to inhabit; it is often "fed" and taken care of so the attendant spirit will aid the owner. Fetishes are used for many purposes, such as hunting, healing, and representing personal totems.

looking, filled with cider. Slips of paper with the words to the songs
are available for each person present.

Number of people needed: Two—a priest and a priestess.

Costumes: Everyone comes in a costume of their choice.

Background Music: Alan Stivell's *Celtic Symphony*

THE RITUAL

As the group enters the circle, one of them reads:

Hey, Ho, for Hallowe'en!
Then the Witches shall be seen.
Some in black, and some in green.
Hey, Ho, for Hallowe'en!
Horse and hattock, horse and go,
Horse and pellatis, ho! ho!

—English folk song

Invoke the elements. Priest/Priestess closes circle, saying:

Bridget, Bride, Our Lady Bright!
Harvest Mother, Queen of Night!
Horned Hunter, Cernunnos, Herne!
Be with us as the year doth turn!

Priestess: **Now is the ending and beginning of the year. As the
snake does curl upon itself and make a never-ending circle, so
does the year complete the sacred cycle of birth, death, and rebirth. The Lady has given us the last of the harvest and gathered
in the bounty of her fertile fields. Now will she sleep until the
season calls her back to once more birth the Lord of the Sun.
Then she will melt the icy crown of the Hunter and garland him
with love knots as she brings in the spring.**

**But now the veils between the worlds are thinnest, and the
Lady walks between them to take her rest. Snow will blanket
her and keep her safe in the arms of the Earth while the**

Hunter is abroad. For now is the time of wintery nights and cold moons touched by tattered clouds.

Priest: I am the father of all that is.
Many are my Names:
I am the Master of the Animals,
Keeper of the woodlands and trees.
I am Sky-Rider and Storm-Bringer;
I wield the lightning bolt.
I forge the sword's steel;
I guide the arrow's path.
Hawks sit at my wrist;
Stags bound beside me.
I am the double-faced gatekeeper;
I am the triple guardian.
I spark the flames of Life;
I lead to the darkness of Death.
I am the strength of the oak;
I am crowned with horns of power.
I am son, lover, and sacrifice;
I am the father of all that is.

Now is my dark season come, when I take up the bow and hunting horn and lead the Wild Hunt across stormy skies. Beware of riding in my train now, for my touch can both inspire and make mad. Only those who travel to the Gates of Death are assured a safe journey. Others must take their chances if they join my wild ride. But, if you would dare (pause) if you have courage (pause) if you would take my hand (pause), you might learn the languages of the animals. You might see the Faery Folk and dance a round[6] with them. You might listen and learn the secrets of the Wind. You might lift the veil of the Moon and

---

[6]A round is a circular formation or ring of dancers, usually holding hands. This form of dance was used in European Maypole dancing and can be seen reflected in children's dances such as "Round the Mulberry Bush."

know the beauty of her smile. You might ride the night on a great stag's back. You might hear music from a castle dark and dead. You might even be brought back safe and sound to your own bed (pause) with only the dim memory of a horn's blast, a far-away hunting cry, and, if a maid, perhaps the lingering hint of a kiss upon your lips.

So make your choice and ride the night with me,
If magical, wondrous sights you would see.
Some I'll leave behind; others I will bless:
Which I'll do for you, is only your guess.
With baying hound and horn the Wild Hunt flies;
Herne the Hunter rides the dark midnight skies!
Upon my wrist there sits a falcon bold,
With bright eyes like amber, set into gold.

The Priestess takes the basket of fetishes and raises them high, saying:

Hail, Herne! Mighty Lord of the Forests, Dread Guardian of the Gates of Life and Death, Gentle love of our Lady.

May the Stag of Herne give you sustenance while the world lies frozen, and may his antlers protect you and keep the chill of winter from your heart.

Pass the basket so all may take a deer figure; while passing the basket, the group chants and claps their hands:

Argludd[7] Herne! Argludd Herne!

When all have taken a deer, a circle dance begins while the Priestess chants:

Harvest home, the Lady sleeps.
The Spring's promise the Earth keeps!
Winter's cold, the Hunt does ride!

---

[7]Pronounced *Ar-glooth*: Welsh for *Lord*.

Best for all to stay inside!
Now's the time Old Herne is seen!
Hey, Ho, Hey, for Hallowe'en!

The dance stops. The chalice is passed while the group sings in a round:

Lady, weave your circle tight
Spin a web of growing light.
Earth and Air and Fire and Water
Bind us to her.

Master, lead your Hunt tonight
Bathed in your Lady's silver light.
Earth and Air and Fire and Water
Ride in your train.

Dismiss the elements; thank Bridget and Herne. Group leaves circle singing:

Merry do we meet, and merry part,
Peace in our souls, joy in our hearts.
Circle is broken; feasting can begin.
Merry do we part, to meet again.

DIRECTIONS

Clay is an inexpensive and effective way to make gifts to be given away during a ritual. We have made Goddess figures, animal fetishes, and spirals for pendants or earrings out of clay. We use high-fire stoneware and terra-cotta for our pieces and either cover them with iron oxide or smoke fire them much the same way the American Indians of the Southwest do. Iron oxide is very simple; it gives an attractive, earthy finish without having to deal with glazes.

You can purchase clay from a pottery supply house, and sometimes you can get a place that deals in poured ceramics to fire a piece for you. Most colleges offer courses in ceramics and pottery; this will give you access to a gas kiln and let you make whatever you want. If you don't want to take a ceramics course and don't have access to a kiln, you might try some of the art "clays" that can be purchased at craft stores. These can often be fired in your kitchen oven or just dried in the open air.

You can carve shapes and designs on your figures, decorate them with beads, feathers, or fur—use your imagination. Sometimes we make the figures ahead of time and pass them out during the ritual; other times we let the participants make the figures as part of the ritual, returning the pieces to the guests after firing or drying.

Another use of clay is to make symbols of things you want to let go of or release from your life. Leave the piece unfired and place it outside where the elements can wear it away and take the clay back into the earth. As the clay dissolves, so will the thing or force it represents.

The deer fetishes we used here were very simple. Shape the clay into what represents the shape of a deer to you, then take a needle or toothpick and poke a hole in the top of the head. After the clay is dried or fired, bend copper wire into the shape of antlers and glue the antlers into the hole. You can decorate the fetish with pieces of real antler if you wish. Some simple circle dances are described in Appendix B.

VARIATIONS

The words of the priest and priestess are the most important parts of this ritual; if you need to make it a little shorter, you can leave off the recitation at the beginning and the singing at the end. For a group with little or no ritual experience, you might consider leaving out the chant and circle dance. For a group with more experience that would like to be more involved, you might try passing out the words to the chant used during the circle dance and have everyone say it together.

Samhain Ritual #2
by Veronica

Audience: This ritual was originally done as a taped presentation; because of this, there was no audience participation or interaction, no invocations, no decorations or props—just the main text of the ritual.

Purpose: The purpose of this ritual was to celebrate the Goddess coming into her aspect as Crone, accenting both the sadness at the death of the God and the coming of winter, and the understanding that this is a necessary part of Nature's cycle. This is a meditative ritual, designed to make the audience realize and respect the wisdom and power of the Crone.

Number of people needed: Two; although the text could be read by one person, it really takes two people to get the rhythm right. The Priestess should come in right as the Priest stops, "biting off" his last syllables. Likewise, the Priest should come in on top of the Priestess's last syllables.

Background Music: None. This ritual is most effective done in complete silence.

THE RITUAL

Priestess: **I am the Crone, the keeper of wisdom, mistress of magic, keeper of riddles. The knowledge I own I have gained from pain and from joy. Once I wore the Maiden's white and the Queen's red cloak, but the flowers have withered, and the King is dead.**

Priest: **The black of night**

Priestess: **I take up.**

Priest: **The hue of death**

Priestess: **I take up.**

Priest: **The cold of winter**

Priestess: **I take up.**

Priest: **The cloak of sleep**

Priestess: **I take up.**

Priest: **The crown of wisdom**

Priestess: **I take up.** (pause) **The Earth opens at my command; the blackness gapes before me. In the underworld, the sorrow-world, my love waits behind the locked and bolted gates. But the power is mine. Through pain have I gained the answer to the riddle, and the gates yield before me.**

Priest: **Cloaked in black**

Priestess: **I descend.**

Priest: **Crowned with wisdom**

Priestess: **I descend.**

Priest: **Through the ice**

Priestess: **I descend.**

Priest: **To the world of sleep**

Priestess: **I descend.**

Priest: **To the realm of death**

Priestess: **I descend.** (pause) **I ascend the throne of Queen of the Night. I, who once ruled beside the Sun, now oversee his exile. I, the Lady of Light, now blacken my face. Once I gave life to the Earth; now I smite my children with violent storms.**

Priest: **The black raven**

Priestess: **I command.**

Priest: **Herald of death**

Priestess: **I command.**

Priest: **Bringer of dreams**

Priestess: **I command.**

Priest: **Rider of north winds**

Priestess: **I command.**

Priest: **Croaker of wisdom**

Priestess: **I command.**

Priest: **On this night, the first and the last, the Wheel turns to darkness, the Moon hides her face, the Sun lies in the grave. Soon the Earth will be wrapped in snow, in sleep.**

Priestess: **My children cry out from pain and from fear. They will learn, as I have learned, that life demands death, the crop must be plowed under for new growth to come. The path of my knowledge is a hard one. Mark my steps and follow, as the Wheel spins on.**

VARIATIONS

Most likely, you will want to add invocations to the elements and the Crone Goddesses (Hecate, Arianrhod, etc.). For decorations, you can either use symbols of death and darkness (a black cloth on the altar, minimum candlelight, bones, dried or withered flowers) or just keep the altar bleak and bare. One custom our group has used in the past is to save the crown of flowers from the Maypole to use as an altar centerpiece for Samhain, and then burn it during the ritual to represent the death of summer. A dark, bitter red wine or juice (like cranberry) in the chalice would fit the theme.

To add more action to this ritual, you can have the priest drape the priestess with a black mantel or cape during their first exchange, and paint her face with black spirals during their second exchange. You may want to pass symbols of the Crone (small bones? crow's feathers?), saying something like, "Take this symbol of the Crone's power, and accept the wisdom she offers." If you have enough people, you can have more than one person read the priest's part, but this might take a little practice to get the rhythm down.

Chapter 3

Yule

───────────── **December 22** ─────────────

Jul   **Iul**   **Winter Solstice**

Yule is a holiday that comes to us from the Norse and Teutonic peoples. Yule (from the Old Norse *iul*, meaning *wheel*) was the major holiday for the Norse, being the day when the sun begins to grow stronger and signals the coming of the end of winter. Yule is the Old Norse New Year, which is the reason our own New Year falls near the winter solstice.[1]

The Norse god Freyr, associated with the sun, presided over Yule along with the Earth Goddess Nerthus. Boars, sacred to Freyr, were sacrificed at this time (hence the origin of "The Boar's Head Carol") as well as horses. The most important rite of this time was the Yule Log, a log brought into the house and kept burning all night in honor of Thor or Freyr. Ashes from the Yule Log were scattered in the fields to ensure a good harvest, and some were kept in the house as protective charms. A tiny piece of the Yule Log was saved to kindle the log the following year.

---

[1]The exact dates of the solstices and equinoxes vary slightly from year to year; an almanac or astrological calendar will list the exact dates each year.

Figure 4. Yule.

Yule is also the time of year when the Wild Hunt was most active. Woden (in Germany) or Herne (in England) rode through the sky on stormy winter nights, leading the souls of dead warriors on the Hunt. Whoever was foolish enough to be out this night was caught up by Woden and forced to join the Hunt, sometimes never to be seen again. Interestingly enough, our modern, friendly, winter spirit Santa Claus owes part of his origin to these old Pagan gods of storms and death. "Nik" was another name for Woden, and in the earlier stories, "Saint Nick" rides Woden's white horse through the sky.

Some of our more familiar Christmas customs come from earlier rituals. "Wassailing," now used to mean "caroling," was a custom where cider or wassail was offered to a particular tree in each apple orchard, and songs were sung to it in order to ensure a good crop of apples the next season. Our modern fascination with mistletoe at Christmastime harkens back to the time when the Druids gathered the sacred mistletoe at Yule, and people hung it in their doorway to protect their homes from lightning and fire. Kissing under the mistletoe springs from an old belief that if a young woman could get a young man to follow her under a patch of mistletoe, he was sure to marry her.

Our modern associations of deer with Christmas stem from the "Stag Dance," "Horn Dance," or the "Dancing of the Horn," an ancient ritual of the winter solstice representing the hunting or the expulsion of the winter spirit. This same theme is found in the British tradition of the "Hunting of the Cutty Wren," still performed in some parts of Britain today. These rituals remind us that in the dead of winter, the sun is reborn; that life is present even in the height of death's power. This spark of life, this power of regeneration is also symbolized in the Mummer's Plays that are traditionally performed at this time. In most of the plays, Saint George fights the Turkish Knight, and one of them is killed. By the intervention of the Doctor, the dead warrior is brought back to life, even as the sun is restored to life on this night.

It is at Yule that we can still see vestiges of the myth of the Oak King and the Holly King. These two brothers are locked in an eternal struggle for power. The Holly King, the spirit of winter, rules from Samhain to Beltane, while the Oak King, the spirit of summer, rules the light half, from Beltane to Samhain. The Oak King is born at Yule, comes into power at Beltane with his marriage to the Goddess, and is killed by his brother at Lammas. The symbols still in use at Christmas today reflect this myth. Holly decorations represent the power of the Holly King at its height, while mistletoe, which was always most sacred when found growing on oak trees, symbolizes the rebirth of the Oak King and his coming return to power. The ivy, of "The Holly and the Ivy," is the Goddess who gives birth to the Oak King and sustains him in his infancy.

The significance of Yule lies in the eternal cycle of death and rebirth; even during the longest night of the year, we can anticipate the return of the sun in its glory. The God of Summer and the God of Winter are twins, aspects of the same power, as are life and death. At Yule, we celebrate both the power of the Holly King—the spirit of death—and the birth of the Oak King—the spirit of life. Here we can better understand the Crone's riddle: the height of power contains the seeds of destruction, and the darkest night is the birthday of the sun.

Yule Ritual
by Janice

Purpose: The point of this ritual was to emphasize the turning of the Wheel of the Year and celebrate the rebirth of the Sun.

Decorations: Decorate the circle in red and green. Have holly and mistletoe on the altar, and a Yule Log decorated with ribbons and candles. A figure of a stag or boar should also be at the altar.

Necessary props: A wooden or ceramic bowl should be filled with small rounds of antlers scrimshawed with an eight-spoked Yule Wheel. There should be dark red wine in the chalice. One small, unlit candle (a 3 inch taper) for everyone present; a Squire or Maiden can pass these out as people enter the circle. (You may also want to use small cardboard "wax catchers" if you do not have a circle cloth.) There should be enough mistletoe for each participant to take a small sprig home.

Number of people needed: A minimum of two, but six works better: the opening lines are more effective if they are done by different voices and come from different places around the circle.

Costumes: None.

Background Music: Use a rhythmic, tribal music such as "Bones" or "Totem" by Gabrielle Roth.

THE RITUAL

Invocations to the elements and the God and Goddess are placed in the middle of the ritual for effect. The circle begins in total darkness. All lights are out, including any Christmas tree lights. The people enter in silence. The first words are spoken in darkness, the voices coming from different places around the circle:

Voice 1: Darkness (pause) **Total** (pause) **Complete** (pause) **Enfolding** (pause).

Voice 2: Black as a raven's wing.

Voice 3: Soft as wool.

Voice 4: Hard as the edge of a sword blade.

Voice 5: Only one faint glimmer of light shines in hope and promise.

The Priestess lights a single candle, saying:

This circle is closed and consecrated in the names of Herne and Bridget, Woden and Frigg.

The Wheel that holds the seasons of the year has turned to the Dark Time, and the weight of winter lies heavy on the land. The Dark Mother, the Wise One, the Crone, pulls her cloak about her as she casts the bones of fate to see who will survive the lean and hungry time.

The Dark Lord, the GateKeeper, the Hunter, hones his steel and calls the hunting cry as he rides the land, bidding those who will not see the spring to come and ride the Hunt with him.

The land lies asleep under its blanket of ice and snow. Fox and badger prowl the ragged edges of the forest. The stag shakes the frozen breath from his lips and starts at the call of the wolf. All await the coming of the returning light: all await the birth of the Sun.

For now it is that the Great Mother does give birth to the Sun King. And he, in his light and splendor, will turn the Great Wheel and start the lengthening of the days that will return the spring and the warmth.

The Hunter will change his crown of holly to one of oak, and the Mother will shed her dark robes for a green one of quickening life.

Join now with the badger and the fox, the stag and the Land, the Crone and the Hunter, as the Wheel is turned.

The Priestess takes her candle and lights the candle of the person on her left, who in turn lights the candle of the person on her left, and so on, so the flame passes clockwise around the circle. As the Priestess lights the first candle, she begins to chant, and each person joins in as his or her candle is lit:

The Solstice fires burn!
The Sun King returns!

When all candles are lit, each person holds his or her candle in one hand and reaches the other hand toward the center of the circle, forming one spoke of the Wheel. When the Wheel is formed, everyone circles clockwise around the altar, continuing the chant. When the Wheel has turned threes times and the Priestess comes back to her place, she stops the dance, saying:

It is done!
The Sun King is reborn!
The Oak Reign begins!

The cauldron is now lit, and the elements are invoked:

Earth: **Spirits of Earth, join us as we celebrate the return of the Sun.**

Air: **Spirits of Air, join us as we celebrate the return of the Sun.**

Fire: **Spirits of Fire, join us as we celebrate the return of the Sun.**

Water: **Spirits of Water, join us as we celebrate the return of the Sun.**

The Priestess now invokes the God and Goddess, saying:

Gentle Lord and Gracious Lady, join us as we celebrate the return of the Sun.

The Priestess takes up the bowl of antler rounds saying:

A gift from the brow of Herne, the Horned Lord of the Forests, Master of the Greenwood. May it remind you of the eight-spoked Wheel of the Year and the sacred days that mark them.

She passes the basket, saying:

May Herne protect you during the remaining time of cold and frost.

As the basket is passed, the group begins to sing "Invocation."[2] The song stops as the basket returns to the Priestess. The Priestess then passes the chalice while everyone sings "Lady Weave" in a round.

Dismiss elements. The Priestess thanks the Lord and Lady, saying:

Woden, Hooded Wise One.
Frigg, Mother of Gods and Men.
Bridget, Lady of the Forge.
Herne, Master of the Greenwood.
We thank you for your gift of Light!

The group leaves the circle, singing "Merry Meet, Merry Part."

DIRECTIONS

Wax catchers: Many craft or candle stores sell ready-made wax catchers, but they are very easy to make. Simply take some poster board or other lightweight cardboard and cut it into small circles or squares (your choice: both work equally well), about three or four inches across. Then cut a slit from one edge into the center of the circle (square), and cut a small hole in the center at the end of the slit. You should be able to slide the candle easily but snugly in the slit and into the hole in the center. When properly done, the wax catcher will grip the candle tightly all by itself. You might want to experiment a little and make sure your candles fit in the wax catchers before you make them in quantity.

    Scrimshaw: Scrimshaw is the ancient art of bone carving. In scrimshaw, designs are etched into polished pieces of bone or antler and stained with red ochre or black India ink. You will need some bone or antler, a fine-toothed saw, sandpaper, soft suede, etching tools, and red ochre or black India ink. If you don't like using animal bone or horn, you can also scrimshaw with "vegetable ivory," or ivory nuts. These hard seeds from South American palm trees can be treated exactly like bone or antler. Your lapidary shop will probably have them or be able to tell you where to find them.

---

[2]For complete text and music of songs, see appendix A on page 111.

First, use the saw to cut your piece of bone or antler to the correct length and smooth off any rough edges with the sandpaper. When you have it shaped the way you want, polish the surface to be carved using progressively finer grades of sandpaper. When the surface feels smooth and slick, use the soft leather to polish it until it is very shiny. The smoother the surface, the sharper your image will be.

When the surface is as slick and as shiny as you can make it, it is time to carve your design. You may want to draw your design with a pencil first to see how it looks and give you a guideline to follow; the pencil can be wiped off with your finger. When you are satisfied with the design, take an etching tool, such as a large sewing needle or a sharp probe, and scratch your design onto the polished surface of the bone. Be very careful when etching because every scratch you make is going to absorb the ink. When the design is finished, rub India ink over the scratches and wipe off any excess with a soft rag.

Before you work on your design, you'll probably want to try a test piece with one or two scratches to see if the surface is polished enough. Working on the marrow or core of the antler is sometimes hard as it is difficult to polish smooth enough. It is very absorbant and can take too much of the ink, blurring your design. Having a well-polished surface is the key to having the piece come out well.

You can drill a small hole through the piece if you want to make a pendant out of it. Antler sliced crosswise and decorated can make a nice necklace. You can often find antlers at antique stores or flea markets. If you live around deer and know where to look, you might find shed antlers, that is, antlers that the deer shed each year. Shed antlers will have an extra, rounded knob at the end while antlers taken by hunters will be sawed off flat.

Cow bones and horns can be used instead of antler; they will polish very well. Also, cow horns can be decorated with a wood-burning iron; if carefully done, it is very difficult to tell a burned-in design from a scrimshawed one.

VARIATIONS

To emphasize the "dark becoming light" theme, the circle begins in total darkness, and the elements and deities are not invoked until the very end of the ritual. If this does not feel right to you, you might try doing a brief invocation to the elements and the Lord and Lady at the beginning of the ritual; to preserve the effect of the ritual, simply say the words without lighting any candles or the cauldron. Also, any initial invocations should have the idea of "Help us through the dark time." Then, you can invoke the elements and the God and Goddess with candles and cauldron later.

As always, the singing can be left out, or you can slip in favorite songs from your own group. The "Wheel Dance" is not very difficult and it is very effective; unless your group, for whatever reason, will not dance, we recommend you try it at least once.

Chapter 4

Imbolg

──────── February 2 ────────		
Oimelc	Brigantia	Candlemas
Bride's Day	St. Brigid's Day	Groundhog Day

The festival of Bridget, Brigid, Brigantia, Ffraid, Brid, Bri'id (rhymes with *breed*), or Bride is the celebration of the return of the Maiden of Spring. Now the Crone undergoes her wonderful transformation into the beautiful Maiden of Flowers, Mistress of the Hunt. Imbolg[1], meaning "in the belly," is the start of the lambing season, the first sign of returning life, the quickening of the year. As a symbol of the returning spring, serpents were said to wake from their winter sleep and venture out of their holes on Bride's Day. Imbolg is the festival of light in the darkness, the celebration of rekindled fire.

Bridget is the Celtic Goddess of the Forge, a fire goddess who rules over inspiration, healing, and poetry as well as smithcraft. Both as a saint and a goddess, she is triple-aspected as the patroness of healers, craftsmen, and poets; sometimes she appeared as three sisters all named Bridget, with different functions assigned to each. Bards were sacred to Bridget, and they were given consecrated bells at Imbolg to tie around their walking staffs in her honor. There is evidence that the medieval

---

[1]Pronounced *im-mol'g*, with the hint of a vowel sound between the *l* and the *g*.

Figure 5. Candlemas.

cult of the Virgin Mary grew out of the cult of Bridget. This theory is supported by the appellation of "St." Bridget as "the Celtic Mary," and by the practice in some churches of having the regular ordination ceremony in the chapel, and then taking the novitiates to an underground vault for a "secret" ordination. (There are letters to Irish abbots from continental bishops condemning such practices; similar traditions were carried on in England, Scotland, and even the Cathedral at Chartres.) It is probable that the first recipient of courtly love songs was none other than Bridget, Goddess of Inspiration, patroness of bards.

Bridget is also worshipped as the Goddess of Hearth and Home. On the eve of Imbolg in Scotland, the women of the house would dress up a sheaf of oats and lay it in a basket (called "Bri'id's bed") along with a phallic-shaped club. They would light candles around the "bed," chanting, "Bri'id is come! Bri'id is welcome!" The candles would be left burning all night. The next morning, if an impression in the shape of the club appeared in the ashes of the fireplace, it was a sign that Bri'id had visited the house and heralded a fruitful, prosperous year.

Our modern Groundhog Day dates back to another northern European custom associated with Imbolg, that of watching the weather to determine what the rest of the winter would be like. In Germany, the badger was watched for weather divination. When settlers from Germany came to the United States, they couldn't find any badgers in their area, so they started watching groundhogs instead.

Imbolg Ritual #1
by Janice

Audience: This ritual was originally done for our regular group and guests, but we have also used it as a presentation for a women's spirituality group at a local Unitarian Church.

Purpose: This ritual celebrates the first stirrings of spring and the festival of Bridget as the Triple Goddess.

Decorations: Have many candles and a cauldron with a large candle in it at the center of the altar. (Note, the cauldron is *not* lit!) Scatter flowers, bones, and fruit around the altar. We also had a small *Bridget's Cross*[2] as part of the centerpiece.

Necessary props: One white, one red, and one black candle around the cauldron. A large green candle for Herne. Have three baskets on the altar: one filled with fresh flowers, one filled with fruit, and one filled with tiny clay spirals. White wine in the chalice.

Number of people needed: Four—one priestess and three maidens.

Costumes: One maiden should wear white with flowers in her hair to represent the "Maiden" aspect of the Goddess. One should wear red and carry a sheaf of wheat as the "Mother" aspect. The third should wear black with a veil over her face as the "Crone" aspect.

Background Music: "From the Goddess," by On Wings of Song and Robert Gass.

THE RITUAL

Priestess: **I declare this space closed and consecrated in the names of the Triple Goddess who is one, and Herne the Hunter.**

Invoke elements.

Priestess: **This is the celebration of Candlemas, the feast of returning light and the festival of purification. We nurture the flames born at the winter solstice as the days turn upward into spring. Winter and death shall be swept away and banished, until the Wheel turns once again to their time of rest and repose. Now is the quickening of the year and new life stirs in the**

---

[2]An Irish folk-art cross made of rushes or straw and woven into an equal-armed cross with a plaited center. The arms are tied off with the ends left loose. The crosses were traditionally made once a year at Imbolg when the old ones were burnt. Some believe the Bridget's Cross is derived from a pre-Christian practice that prepared the seed for planting each spring.

womb of the Great Mother. This is the feast of poets, and is sacred to the Goddess in her triple aspect. Hear now the words of the Goddess in her first aspect.

The "Maiden" comes forth holding the basket of flowers.

Maiden: **I am the white maid of enchantment and creativity. I am inception and expansion. I am the waxing phase of the moon and from my fingertips come the flowers that herald the spring. I am new leaves. I am gentle rain. I am soft sunshine. I am the whisper of wings. I am Persephone. I am Kore. I am Bri'id. I am the fresh beginnings of new life.**

The Maiden lights the white candle at the altar and gives a flower to everyone, saying:

Accept my gift. Accept the life of Spring.

Priestess: **Hear now the words of the Goddess in her second aspect.**

The Mother comes forward, holding the basket of fruit.

Mother: **I am the Crimson Mother of ripeness and fertility. I am stability and fulfillment. I am the full phase of the moon and from my womb comes the bounty and richness of summer. I am bursting fields. I am moist earth. I am ripening corn. I am the warmth of the home fires seen from a distant hill. I am Demeter. I am Gaia. I am Danu. I am the rich center of life.**

She lights the red candle at the altar and gives fruit to everyone saying:

Accept my gift. Accept the bounty of the Mother.

Priestess: **Hear now the words of the Goddess in her third aspect.**

The Crone comes forward, holding the basket of spirals.

Crone: **I am the dark Grandmother of Time. I am wisdom and knowledge. I am the waning phase of the moon and from my bones come the silence and the cold of winter. I am black nights. I am the coiling snake. I am the howl of the wolf. I am the tomb. I am Hecate. I am Kali. I am the Morrigan. I am the keeper of the Sacred Spiral. I am the Ending before the Beginning.**

She lights the black candle at the altar and gives spirals to everyone, saying:

Accept the gift of the Crone and know the secret of the Spiral.

Priest lights the green candle at the altar.

Priestess: **We welcome the Lord of the Hunt, Herne, Master of the Greenwood.**
   Without light there is no dark; without the dark, no light. Without spring there comes no summer; without summer, no winter; without winter, no spring.
   The Spiral represents the process of creation and birth. It is the passage from the hidden to the seen. It is the symbol of the Goddess of Creation and it is the combined knowledge of the Maiden, the Mother, and the Crone. Through it may you come to know the light of birth, the fullness of life, and the transformation of death.

Everyone holds the spirals in their right hand and charges them with energy, chanting:

Isis, Astarte, Diana,
Hecate, Demeter, Kali,
Inanna

Continue the chant while the Crone leads everyone in a spiral dance. When everyone returns to their place, the Priestess passes the chalice while the group sings:

We all come from the Maiden
And to her we shall return
Like the budding flowers
Blooming in the springtime.

We all come from the Mother
And to her we shall return
Like a grain of wheat
Falling to the reaper's scythe.

We all come from the Wise One
And to her we shall return
Like the waning moon
Shining on the winter snow.

Thank and dismiss the elements, and the God and Goddess.

Priestess: **Our circle is open but not broken. Merry Meet, Merry Part — let the feasting begin!**

DIRECTIONS
The "spiral dance" can be done in various ways. Basically, everyone joins hands, and one person leads the group around the circle clockwise, spiraling in towards the center. You can either wind the spiral tight, then drop hands and reform the circle, or you can wind the spiral loosely so that the leader has room to turn and unwind the spiral with no one dropping hands. The spiral dance can be slow and stately or quick and raucous; we have even had the leader take us (running!) around the entire house and form the spiral in another room. Then, we were led back to the circle to finish the ritual, everyone breathless and laughing. One word of warning on a "raucous" dance, however: make certain your path is clear so no one trips!

To make the clay spirals, take a piece of clay and roll it on a table until it looks like a worm or snake. Then, coil it into a spiral. If you wish, you can flatten the "snake" with a rolling pin before you start to coil it. Decorate however you wish. You can also make the spirals out of bread dough and bake them.

VARIATIONS

If necessary, one person could play all three Goddesses, but having three different people is very effective. Songs and chants can be left out, or you can substitute your favorite ones instead. If you are having your ritual in a small space, you may want to do a simple circle dance instead of the spiral.

Imbolg Ritual #2
by Veronica

Purpose: This ritual is intended to celebrate the festival of Bridget, so it is dedicated only to her.

Decorations: Circle should be decorated with buds of flowers, if available. All element candles and other candles around the circle should be white.

Necessary props: A cauldron and three large white candles on the altar, ringed with new greenery and budding flowers. Each person gets a small, unlit white candle (a 3 inch taper) and a slip of paper with words to the songs as he or she enters the circle. I used Irish Cream Liqueur in the chalice, because this is the festival when the ewes begin producing milk for the newborn lambs.

Number of people needed: One.

Costumes: None.

Background Music: "Sounds of Nature" tape of a flowing stream.

THE RITUAL
Invoke the elements.

Earth: **Spirits of the empty fields, waiting silently under a blanket of snow, join us in greeting our lady bright.**

Air: **Spirits of the warming winds, blowing ever stronger from the south, join us in greeting our lady bright.**

Fire: **Spirits of the shining flame, burning in the infant Sun, join us in greeting our lady bright.**

Water: **Spirits of the forest streams, breaking free from your prison of ice, join us in greeting our lady bright.**

The Priest/Priestess lights the first altar candle, saying:

Bridget, lady of fire, of hearth and forge, we welcome your return.

The Priest/Priestess lights the second altar candle, saying:

Bride, lady of healing, of peace and joy, we welcome your return.

The Priest/Priestess lights the third altar candle, saying:

Bri'id, lady of inspiration, of vision and poetry, we welcome your return.

Priest/Priestess enters: **Bri'id returns from her winter sleep, Warm Spring follows in her steps.
Soon the trees are green again,
Soon the flowers bloom.
We welcome back our Lady Bri'id
And every house makes room.**

All: **Bri'id is come! Bri'id is welcome!**

Priest/Priestess: **She lays aside her cloak of death
And wakes the world with her sweet breath.**

All: **Bri'id is come! Bri'id is welcome!**

Priest/Priestess: **And in the dark and frozen lands
We joyfully greet the newborn lambs.**

All: **Bri'id is come! Bri'id is welcome!**

Priest/Priestess: **And grateful for this sign of life
We gather here by candlelight.**

All: **Bri'id is come! Bri'id is welcome!**

Priest/Priestess: **And in the depth of winter's blight,
We welcome Bri'id, our lady bright!**

All: **Bri'id is come! Bri'id is welcome!**

Priest/Priestess: **And all her bards will form a ring
And to their Lady Bri'id they sing:**

All: **Bri'id is come! Bri'id is welcome!**

The Priestess takes her candle and lights it at the first altar candle, saying:

Fire of Bridget, keep us warm through the year and fill our homes with love.

The Priestess holds her candle in the flame of the second altar candle, saying:

Fire of Bride, burn away our illnesses and fill our hearts with joy.

The Priestess holds her candle in the flame of the third altar candle, saying:

Fire of Bri'id, shine as our guide and fill our souls with song.

The Priestess then turns to the person on her left and lights his or her candle. The flame passes around the circle to the left as the Priestess and first person begin to sing; each person joins the song as soon as his or her candle is lit:

Bridget of shining fire,
Lady of flickering flame,
Grant us our hearts' desire,
Be with us, we call your name!

After all the candles are lit, the song breaks into a round. After the round is sung three times, it stops. Candles may be blown out when the song stops.

Priestess takes up chalice, saying:

Bridget, Bride, Bri'id, we welcome you into our homes and our hearts. Shine brightly for us, Lady of Fire, that we may always feel your warmth.

Priestess passes chalice while people sing:

Brigid of shining fire,
Lady of flickering flame,
Grant us our hearts' desire,
Be with us, we call your name!

Thank the elements.

Water: **Rejoice, O Spirits of the Stream:**
Bri'id is come! You soon flow free!

Fire: **Spirits of the infant Sun,**
Rejoice — Your Lady Bri'id is come!

Air: **Spirits who ride the warming Air,**
Rejoice — Your Lady Bri'id is here!

Earth: **Rejoice, O Spirits of the Earth:**
Bri'id is here! You soon give birth!

Priestess: **Lady Bri'id, we welcome you into the world once**
again. Our circle is open. Let the feasting begin!

All: **Bri'id is come! Bri'id is welcome!**

VARIATIONS
The easiest way to vary this ritual would be to have two people alternate verses of the chant. We chose not to do that originally because it was easier to have only one person read it. Another variant would be to have three people involved, one reading the invocation to Bridget, one the invocation to Bride, and one the invocation to Bri'id. The Priestess could wear a "Maiden aspect" costume, dressed in white with flowers in her hair. The "Bri'id is Come! Bri'id is welcome!" chant lends itself easily to a circle dance, although a group composed mainly of newcomers may find it difficult to do an irregular chant and a dance at the same time. If you have enough regular members present to lead the chant, a dance would be perfect.

Chapter 5

Ostara

<table>
<tr><td colspan="3" align="center">March 20</td></tr>
<tr>
<td align="center">Oestara
Vernal Equinox</td>
<td align="center">Eostara
Spring Equinox</td>
<td align="center">Easter
Lady Day</td>
</tr>
</table>

Little is given in any sources about the origin and traditions of Ostara. Eostre or Oestre has been referred to as a northern European form of Ishtar or Astarte, although we have seen the same name referring to a hermaphroditic god somehow mysteriously related to the growth of new life. "Eostre" comes from the same root as "east," which may reflect the fact that at the vernal equinox the sun is to the east rather than to the north as it is in winter. In all probability, Eostre was a Germanic or Saxon dawn goddess, her name coming from the same root as the Greek Eos—or Dawn. The egg and the hare were apparently her symbols; red eggs were used at this time as symbols of rebirth and renewal, red being the color of life and dawn. Since "Easter" comes from "Ostara," we should not be surprised to find our Easter symbols originally belonging to Eostre.

In southern Europe, festivals on or about the vernal equinox celebrated the return of the Dying and Rising God (Attis in particular, but Mithras, Tammuz, Adonis, and Osiris as well). To the Greeks, it is the return of Persephone from the underworld, the time when the Earth ceases its period of mourning and new life is seen again. In the old Roman calendar, the beginning of spring was also the beginning of the

Figure 6. Ostara.

year. This is also the time when planting festivals were held to bless the seeds for the coming season.

In the medieval church calendar, the vernal equinox was celebrated as Lady Day or the Feast of the Annunciation, the day when the archangel Gabriel announced to Mary that she would be the mother of Jesus. In northern Europe, Lady Day was traditionally the time when farmers began to hire workers for the imminent planting season.[1] The ideas of the divine incarnation and the preparation for the planting fit very nicely into the theme of rebirth and renewal even as the resurrection of Jesus on Easter follows the theme of the return of the Dying and Rising God.

Both equinoxes are a time of balancing. Now the light has grown in strength and has achieved equal footing with the darkness. Light and dark, masculine and feminine, death and life—all polarities stand in perfect balance. Now is the time to see how well our own souls are balanced, and to plant those things that we are lacking in ourselves.

Ostara Ritual
by Veronica

Purpose: This ritual celebrates the return of the Dying and Rising God, the vegetation god who dies each year at winter and is restored to life again in the spring. The myths and symbols used come from Mediterranean cultures: Greece, Rome, Egypt, Sumeria, and Babylon, where the myth of the Dying and Rising God is most prominent.

Decorations: Lots of flowers upon the altar, and a flower of appropriate color at each direction.

Necessary props: A small basket filled with large seeds (we used gladiolus bulbs) on the altar. A thyrsus should be placed upright in the basket of seeds, and the whole thing draped in a dark cloth.[2]

---

[1] Andrew Rothovius. "Quarter Days and Cross-Quarter Days." *The Old Farmer's Almanac, no. 201: 1993* (Dublin, NH: Yankee Publishing, 1992), p. 50.

[2] The thyrsus is an ancient phallic symbol, originally belonging to the god Dionysus. Covering the thyrsus in a black cloth and revealing it during the ritual is a practice that dates back to the mystery cults of ancient Greece and Rome.

Number of people needed: Two—one Priest and one Priestess. We also depended on the help of two Maidens who taught the chants and circle dance to the group while the Priest and Priestess got into costume.

Costumes: The Priestess should wear a white "spring" dress and flowers in her hair. The Priest should wear bright "natural" colors: reds, greens, purples—anything that suggests the burst of color in the spring.

Background Music: None: there was too much singing in the ritual to have background music.

THE RITUAL

Invoke the elements.

Earth: **Spirits of Earth, spirits of the new-plowed field, join us in our celebration, as we welcome the return of the son from your womb.**

Air: **Spirits of Air, spirits of the warm spring breeze, blow gently across the newborn Earth, carrying the warm spring rains.**

Fire: **Spirits of Fire, spirits of the newborn Sun, return from your exile and warm the dormant seedlings back to life.**

Water: **Spirits of Water, breaking free from your prison of ice, flow into the valleys and bring life to the fields once more.**

Priest/Priestess invokes the God and Goddess, saying:

Osiris, Dumuzi, Adonis, all the world waits for your return. Isis, Inanna, Aphrodite, be with us as we await the return of your love.

Priest: **The equinox is a time of great joy. The young Sun comes of age; the frozen waters break free and begin to flow; the danger of winter is finally past; the hard earth is soft again, and ready to receive the seed.**

Priestess: **The Maiden has returned, trailing flowers in her steps. The reborn earth is ready, prepared for the cycle of life to begin.**

Priest: **But balance in all things is needed: the soil needs the rain, the field, the plow; the ewe, the ram. So the Goddess waits for her Shining Son, The Dying and Rising One.**

The Priestess leads the group in singing:

**Isis waits for Osiris
Inanna for Tammuz
Aphrodite for Adonis
Waiting for her love's return.**

The group continues singing softly while the Priest speaks over them.

**Osiris rules in the Western World.
Adonis waits in the land of the dead.
The Lady wanders the frozen earth,
Mourning for her lover far away.**

The Priest pauses to allow a verse of singing; Priestess stops singing. The Priest begins singing, and gradually the group changes songs (overlapping for a verse or two):

**Tammuz, Adonis, Dumuzi,
Dionysus, Attis, Pelles,
Osiris**

The group continues singing, while the Priestess speaks over them.

Priestess: **But the Sun grows stronger every hour. The winter quickly fades away. Soon the Lady's wait is ended. The time has come for her love's return.**

The Priestess sings:

The Lady waits for her lover
To return from the Western World.
Now the sun grows strong
And the water flows again.

The Lady waits for her lover
To return from the Western World.
Now the warm sun calls
And the world comes back to life.

The Lady waits for her lover
To return from the Western World.
Now the gates swing wide
And the Earth rejoices.

The Priestess stops singing and joins the group in the chant; she also steps back with the people in the circle, leaving the Priest alone in the center. The Priest stops chanting and takes up the basket, saying:

The flowers burst into joyful bloom.
The gentle spring rains come.
The Goddess embraces her Divine Consort,
And we welcome the God to life.

The chant grows louder. The Priest continues:

Attis, Adonis, Osiris, Dumuzi,
We welcome you to the ready earth.
Tammuz, Pelles, Dionysus,
We rejoice at your return.

The Priest uncovers the basket and reveals the thyrsus and the seeds. The Priestess and the group start a circle dance around him, still chanting. The Priest takes up the basket of seeds, saying:

Attis, Adonis, Osiris, Dumuzi,
We ask your help in the coming year.
Tammuz, Pelles, Dionysus,
Enter into these unplanted seeds,
Touch them and fill them with your power.

The dance and chant continue until the Priestess has come around to her place again. Then she calls for a stop and rejoins the Priest at the altar. The Priest hands her the basket of seeds.

Priestess: **Now is the time for sowing and planting. Look within your heart and see the empty spaces waiting to be filled. Take these seeds, touched by the power of the Rising God and plant them in your heart. You need not want for anything.**

Pass basket of seeds. Pass chalice. Dismiss elements, thank the Lord and Lady. Close circle.

DIRECTIONS

The thyrsus was originally a staff wrapped in ivy with an unopened pinecone attached to the top. We needed a smaller version for this ritual—one that could stand up in a basket—so we used a small stick of bamboo (seven or eight inches). Also, we couldn't find an unopened pinecone and wanted a little more green in the ritual anyway, so we used a bright green sprig of juniper instead. We simply wrapped the juniper sprig in thread and tied it to the bamboo. Then we "planted" it in a small cup of soil that sat in the middle of the basket.

Some simple circle dances, including the one we used here, are described in Appendix A.

VARIATIONS

This ritual is very theatrical, a good "grand presentation" for one of my favorite holidays. If the costumes, singing, and dance are too much for you, some of it can be left out. I recommend keeping the background chants if possible, but the priestess' singing parts can easily be spoken, and the seeds can be charged without the dance. If necessary, one person could do the ritual, but that would be a lot to handle.

Chapter 6

Beltane

<table>
<tr><td colspan="3" align="center">May 1</td></tr>
<tr><td>Bealtaine</td><td>Walpurgisdag</td><td>May Day</td></tr>
</table>

"Beltane" translates loosely as "Bel-fire" or "Bel's fire."[1] Bel, Beli, Belenos, or Belinus (in Latin) is the old Celtic god of light and fire, and possibly the sun as well. *Bel* means "bright," and it is probable that this is actually his title or epithet as opposed to his name. Bel is also known as the Bright or Shining One, and some scholars equate him with Lugh, while others translate his name as "lord." Though Bel himself has fallen into mystery, his festival remains the most popular holiday in the British Isles and parts of Europe despite numerous attempts to suppress it, and many of the ancient rites and customs are carried on today in an almost unbroken tradition.

Beltane is a festival of fire and fertility; traditionally, the hearth fire would be kept burning all year until May Eve, when the fire was extinguished and the hearth and chimney were thoroughly cleaned. On the dawn of Beltane, a new fire was kindled in the community hearth. Cattle were driven through the fire to insure their health, protection,

---

[1] In parts of England and Scotland, the Beltane or May Day fires are referred to as "Bale-fires," assumed to be a corruption of the original "Bel-fires."

Figure 7. Beltane.

and fertility, and young men and women jumped through the flames for luck in conceiving children or in catching a spouse. This bonfire was kept burning all day and night; as people returned to their homes, they carried torches from the Beltane fire to rekindle their home fires.

The fertility aspect of Beltane is reflected especially through plants and flowers. Young women would stay out in the woods all night on May Eve making wreaths of May flowers for their hair, gathering hawthorne and other greenery to decorate houses and the village square, and washing in the May morning dew to make themselves beautiful. The young men would find a tree to make the Maypole, a phallic symbol, decorate it with ribbons and greenery, and erect it in the center of the village square. They would then climb the pole and crown it with a garland of flowers. The young people of the village would dance around the Maypole, weaving ribbons up and down it. At Beltane, representatives of the old vegetation god reappear in a somewhat comic way in the person of Jack-in-the-Green or Green George, a prominent figure in May Day games and processions.

A young, unmarried woman was chosen from the village, and she presided over the festival and directed the May Games. Often the May Queen chose a consort from among the young men, or sometimes the young men would compete in a race or a mock combat for the title of May King. The May King and Queen are thought to represent the Lord and Lady, as Beltane is the celebration of the marriage of the God and Goddess. Robin Hood and Maid Marian appear as May King and Queen in early ballads, and the May King and Queen or the priest and priestess of the coven are often referred to as "Robin and Marian."

Beltane is the first day of summer; it opens the light half of the year. It is a celebration of youth, of love, and of fun. The Maypole Dance, jumping through the Beltane bonfire, and the May Day games all celebrate the God coming into his prime. On this day, we celebrate the divine marriage that ensures the fertility of the earth. On Beltane the Goddess changes her aspect from Maiden to Queen and Mother: Persephone becomes Demeter; Brigid becomes Danu. The God also changes his aspect: the Sun King comes down from the sky to rule beside his queen as the Hunter on Earth: the Holly King of Winter falls to the Oak King of Summer.

Beltane is the festival at which the Great Rite is performed. In the Rite, the Priest and Priestess represent the God and Goddess incarnate and consummate the divine marriage so the crops will grow. Today, the Rite is symbolically performed by placing a consecrated knife — or *athame* — into the communal chalice. The symbolic Rite allows the group to partake in a more tangible way, as the charged cup is then passed around the circle.

Beltane Ritual #1

by Janice

Purpose: This ritual celebrates the beginning of summer and the marriage of the Lord and Lady.

Like Samhain, Beltane is usually a big party. We get together at two or three in the afternoon and make wreaths of flowers and ivy for the women and of oak leaves for the men. Before the ritual we select a May King and Queen, and have plenty of games and traditional dances, including a Maypole Dance. We erect a Maypole and decorate it with ribbons, gold balls and silver crescents, and a wreath of oak leaves and flowers. Then we dance around the pole, weaving the ribbons together. After the games and dances are over, we gather in the circle for the ritual.

Rules for some of our favorite May Games are given in Appendix D, and instructions for the Maypole Dance are given in Appendix B.

Decorations: We usually like to have Beltane outdoors if we can. We use lots of flowers and ribbons, white candles, and baskets — anything "summery" and pretty.

Necessary props: The element invocations are slightly different than usual, so you will need different props for them: a flower for earth, a feather for air, a small dish containing one or two tablespoons of powdered cinnamon for fire, and a large shell filled with water for water.

You will also need one gold and one silver cord or ribbon, each about twelve inches long. There should also be one two-foot-long gold cord for each of the men, and one two-foot-long silver cord for each of the women. Have a chalice filled with mead (or honey wine) and a cauldron if you cannot have an outdoor fire. Also, have a plate of Beltane cakes or crescent-shaped cookies on the altar.

Number of people needed: Four—one priest, one priestess, two maidens or squires (one of each is best). You will also need to instruct the four volunteers for the elements before the ritual.

Costumes: Everyone should wear wreaths of ivy and flowers (women) or oak leaves and flowers (men). If this is not possible, at least the priest and priestess should wear them.

Background Music: Any bouncy, spirited Irish or Celtic music. An instrumental tape of jigs or country dances is best. We use songs by The Chieftains, Clannad, Celtic Stone, Gypsy Guerilla Band, etc.

THE RITUAL

The May Queen and May King lead the group in procession into the circle as someone reads:

Robin Hood and Little John
They are both gone to Fair-O
And we will go to the merry greenwood
To see what they do there-O
And for to choose-O
To chase the buck and doe
With heel and toe
Jolly rumble-O
For we were up as soon as any day-O
And for to fetch the Summer home
The Summer and the May-O
For Summer is a-come-O and winter is a-gone-O

—English folk song

Priest/Priestess: **Our circle is closed and consecrated in the names of Bridget — Threefold Lady of Inspiration and Healing — and Herne — The Horned Lord of the Trees and Master of the Hunt.**

Invoke the elements.

Earth (lays a flower at the altar): **With blossom and bough and the greenwood of May, we bring the summer in.**

Air (lays a large feather at the altar): **With warm, moist breaths and whispering winds, we bring the summer in.**

Fire (drops cinnamon into the fire, making it sparkle): **With sunlit sparks of saffron and scarlet flame, we bring the summer in.**

Water (sprinkles water from a shell around the altar): **With glistening drops of May morning dew and rain-fresh days, we bring the summer in.**

Priest/Priestess: **Lady Bridget, Arianrhod,**
Beloved of the Hornèd God,
Dance with us in the silver moonlight,
Join our revels in the Greenwood bright!
On Moonlit heath and forest deep,
Or where your Lady's willows weep,
Horn'd Cernunnos, Robin, Herne,
Be with us as the seasons turn.

Priestess: **I am the fruitful Earth.**
I am the Mistress of Summer.
I am the Shining Orb of the Moon.
I am the Light of the distant stars.

I am the Gateway of Death.
I am the vessel of life.
I am the Green Mother of all.
I am the Lady.

Priest: **I am the vault of the sky.**
I am the Master of Winter.
I am the brilliant flame of the sun.
I am the storm clouds, wild and grey.

I am the Keeper of the Gateway.
I am the Bestower of Death.
I am the Green Man of life;
I am the Hunter.

Priestess: **Through the lonely winter have I slept,**
Bound by enchantments of ice and snow.
The greening life of the world I kept,
While my Greenwood Lord a-hunting did go.

Priest: **The Wild Hunt have I led through storm and wind,**
A hawk at my wrist and lightning in my hand,
But now would I rest and let our ways blend,
For her way and mine are bound close with the land.

Maiden/Squire #1 reads the following lines while Maiden/Squire #2 loops a silver and gold cord around the wrists of the Priest and Priestess:

No casual meeting this, but a magical melding of air and fire.
Forged by the elements of nature in an age long past. Cast of
silver and gold under the light of moon and sun and embodied
in the flesh of woman and man.

Like precious metals poured forth and mingled, each one half
of a timeless passion, each one half of a timeless love.

Silver Moon to golden Sun, darkness to light.
Herne's brow, the Lady's crescent, both shine as bright.

The Priest and Priestess share a chalice.

Priest/Priestess: **As the Horned One did dance for the love of his Lady, let us now dance the summer in.**

The women are linked together with silver cords and the men with gold. The Priest leads the men counterclockwise and the Priestess leads the women clockwise. They weave in and out as they dance.

Priest/Priestess: **We share the cake of Beltane among ourselves and with the Lady and the Hunter. Partake of these cakes with the hope of a fruitful summer, then share a portion with the Sacred Fire.**

Sing "Lady Weave"[2] while the cakes are passed. Each person tosses a small portion of the cake in the cauldron or fire.

Priest/Priestess: **May Bridget bless with health and inspired thought, and may the horns of Herne guard and protect all those who drink the sweetness from the cup of May.**

Sing "Invocation" while chalice is being passed. Dismiss elements. The Priest/Priestess thanks the Lord and Lady, saying:

Gentle Lord of the Forests whose horns spark the fires of love, Gracious Lady of Flame and Forge whose healing warmth surrounds us, we thank you for your presence while a-Maying we did go! Summer is in — let the feasting begin!

The group leaves the circle singing "Merry Meet, Merry Part."

---

[2]For complete text and music of songs, see Appendix A on page 111.

DIRECTIONS

Wreaths: You will need strands of fresh ivy or vine, fresh flowers, florist's tape, scissors, and ribbon in various colors.

Take a strand of ivy or grapevine and cut it the size of your head, leaving at least an inch or so extra on both ends. The wreath should rest slightly above your ears — make it too large and it will fall into your eyes, too small and it will fall off your head. After you have cut the strand the right size, overlap the ends and wrap them tightly with the florist's tape. If you have short strands of ivy, you may have to piece several strands together to make the wreath large enough. Once you have the ring together, try it on again to make sure it still fits. Adjust the size if necessary.

Next, clip off the flowers, leaving about three inches of stem. Fit the flowers around the wreath, arranging them however you like. Wrap the florist's tape around the flower stem and the strand of ivy, binding the two together. Put on as many flowers as you like. (It's best to get your flowers from a store or an available flower garden. Otherwise, you might end up with ragweed flowers instead of daisies. Also, wildflowers are subject to protection in some states, so beware of illegally picking something.)

After you have put on the flowers, decide if you want ribbon on your wreath. You can wind the ribbon around the wreath or simply tie it near the back so it hangs down over your shoulders. Some people choose a color that symbolizes something they want; as they wind their ribbon about their wreath, they wish for whatever they want. If you use ribbed curling ribbon, you can take your scissors and drag the edge sharply down the length of the ribbon to make the edges curl gently. The harder you pull the more it will curl.

Baby's breath and fern look nice on wreaths as do larger flowers such as crysanthemums and daisies. The men sometimes like to keep theirs plain or tie pieces of oak leaves onto them. Our group used to provide a red rose for each of the High Priestesses and one for the May Queen.

The Maypole: Maypoles are fairly simple to construct, and once you invest in one, you can use it year after year. We use an 8-foot tall, 2-inch diameter piece of metal electrical conduit set in a patio umbrella stand weighted with sand. If you want to anchor it directly in the ground, add an extra 1½–2 feet to the length of the pole.

You can decorate the pole by wrapping it with ribbon or crepe paper. You can also make a wreath of oak leaves and flowers to crown the top. Rings draped with greenery and flowers can be put around the pole, or it can be topped with a moon and sun cut from cardboard and decorated with glitter. Use a wide, heavy ribbon or crepe paper for your dancing ribbons. Cut these ribbons almost twice the length of the pole and tape or tie them securely to the top.

After the final Maypole Dance, you can tie off the ribbons and leave them until next year, or you can cut them off and burn them in the Beltane Fire.

VARIATIONS

As in Janice's Hallowe'en ritual, the text read by the Priest and Priestess is the meat of the ritual. The opening text from the folk song and the songs at the end can be left out if necessary, as can the dance. If you have access to a Maypole, you may want to dance the Maypole in the ritual instead of the "weave" dance.

Since this ritual celebrates the marriage of the Goddess and the God, it would be nearly impossible to do it with only one person. However, if you have to, you can rewrite the text in the third person (i.e., "She is the fruitful Earth," "He is the vault of the sky," etc.). Then, when it comes time to tie the cord around the hands of the priest and priestess, you can do it symbolically by looping the cord around any god and goddess figures you have, or tie them around the altar candles.

Beltane Ritual #2
by Veronica

Audience: This ritual was originally done as part of a class project, presented for a large group (approximately thirty people), most of whom had no ritual experience. I couldn't count on any audience participation, especially since some of the people in the audience were not very interested in ritual, and at least one was downright hostile to the idea. For this reason, I made the ritual highly theatrical, with almost no audience participation and elaborate staging to keep their interest. Because I was dealing with a time restriction, I invoked the elements and the God and Goddess before the audience arrived. They walked into a pre-cast circle.

Purpose: The main purpose of this ritual was to celebrate Beltane as the marriage of the Goddess and God, the balance of male and female. Its secondary purpose was to introduce Wicca to thirty people who had barely heard of it. It went very well, even better than I'd hoped, and I would recommend this ritual or one like it for a group of newcomers.

Decorations: Because we had to travel with them, and because the people there would not necessarily understand the symbolism, we kept the decorations to a minimum—a crystal ball and silver crescent to symbolize the Goddess; a sun-face plaque and an arrow to symbolize the God; appropriate symbols at each direction for the elements.

Necessary props: The most important props were a large chalice filled with cider and an *athame* (consecrated knife). I used apple juice in the chalice and made sure I had a small towel or cloth to clean the knife. You will also need a white candle for the Goddess and a yellow or gold one for the God. Have an extra red and green candle on the altar. Everyone present received a small, unlit white candle (a 3 inch taper) as they entered the circle. A larger white candle (an 8 or 9 inch taper) should be on the altar. The cauldron was placed a few feet away from the altar near the maiden, and four dishes with appropriate herbs for each element were nearby.

Number of people needed: Three—one priest, one priestess, and one maiden or squire.

Costumes: The priestess wore a silver sash, and had a red sash on the altar. The priest wore a yellow headband, and had a green one on the altar.

Background music: None; we had no tape or sound system available.

THE RITUAL

As the people are led into the circle by the Maiden, the Priest is seated at south and the Priestess is seated at north. The people walk in and sit two feet from the edge of the circle, so the Priest and Priestess can walk around behind them. When everyone is settled, the Priestess stands and says:

I am the huntress who rides the night.
I am the Maiden arrayed in flowers.
I am the Mistress of Earth and Sea.
I am the ruler of the growing land.

The Priestess dances around the circle while the Priest sings "Lady Weave." When the Priestess returns to north, she sits down again. Once the Priestess takes her seat, the Priest stands and says:

I am the rider of the sun-shod horse.
I am the lord of shining fire.
I am the Master of Wind and Flame.
I am the ruler of the open sky.

The Priest dances around the circle while the Priestess sings "Master Lead." The Priest and Priestess do a "chase-dance" around the circle during the following speeches:

Priest: **Come with me and rule the sky,**
And fire and brilliance be,
And I will show you all the things
That the rising sun can see.

Priestess: **Why should I leave the growing land**
And relinquish my own rule?
Come with me—if your heart so moves—
And rule the earth and sea.
And we will ride the skies at night,
And dwell in the deep black caves.

Priest: **Such a thing I cannot do,**
For I will surely die.
But I will run the woods with you,
My fires will warm your lands—
My gentle winds caress your cheek,
If you will but take my hand.

The Priest steps into the center of the circle and holds out his hand to the Priestess. As she says the following lines, she joins him in the center and takes his hand:

And I will show you all the realms
Where the whispered places hide,
And welcome you to my arms at night,
Where you will safely lie.

The Priest and Priestess hold hands over the altar and circle around it as they say the following lines together:

Together we shall hunt the wood
And rule the earth and air,
And all the world shall feel the love
Of the Lord and Lady fair.

The Priestess takes off the silver sash and puts on the red one, saying:

I cast away my maiden days
And take on your radiant hue—
This change will I gladly make
That I may be with you.

The Priest takes off the yellow/gold headband and puts on the green one, saying:

**I lay aside my fiery crown
And take up one of green—
This change will I gladly make
If you will be my queen.**

The Priestess takes the white candle and lights the red one from it; she blows out the white candle and puts the red one in its place on the altar. The Priest does the same with the yellow and green candles.

Priestess: **And so we grow—**

Priest: **Each for the other—**

Priestess: **Maiden to Queen—**

Priest: **Sun-King to Hunter.**

Maiden/Squire: **Now the flames of summer come, burning away winter's chill. God and Goddess reign as one, no longer to be alone. With this flame we welcome summer, and greet the divine pair.** (Lights the cauldron.)

The Priestess takes up the chalice and the Priest takes up the knife.

Priestess: **And so we come—**

Priest: **Each to the other—**

Priestess: **As sword to the cauldron—**

Priest: **As river to sea—**

Priestess: **As lance to grail—**

Priest: **As sun to earth—**

Priest and Priestess: **As man to woman—so mote it be!**

The Priestess holds up the chalice; the Priest places the knife in the chalice and holds it there.

The Maiden/Squire puts appropriate herbs in the cauldron, saying:

The love of the Lord and Lady ignites the elements: warming the earth (puts earth herbs in cauldron); **filling the air** (puts air herbs in cauldron), **burning in fire** (puts fire herbs in cauldron), **glinting off water** (puts water herbs in cauldron). **All are united, and we are one with them.**

The Priest and Priestess put the chalice and knife down.[3] They take the 8 inch white candle and together light it from the cauldron. They light the Maiden's candle, and she lights the candle of the person on her left, saying:

May the light of the summer fire go before and burn within us.

The Priest and Priestess sing "Lady Weave" in a round while the flame is passed to the left. They stop singing, share the chalice, then pass it to the Maiden, and she passes it to the left. When the chalice has gone around:

Priestess: **As the fire will soon die**

Priest: **So the summer will soon pass**

Priestess: **Only to return again**

---

[3]You may want to wipe the knife clean as you set it down; otherwise, it will get wine or juice all over the floor. If this is not possible, set the knife on the cloth and clean it after the ritual.

Priest: **In the cycle of the seasons.**

Priestess: **Setting and rising**

Priest: **Death and life**

Priestess and Priest: **All are one — as the Wheel spins on.**

DIRECTIONS

The "chase-dance" was done as follows: the priest starts out at south, and the priestess at north. When the priest makes his first proposal ("Come with me . . ."), he moves counter-clockwise around to north, while the priestess backs away to west. The priestess continues to move away to south while she rejects his proposal ("Why should I leave . . ."). She stops at south and reverses direction as she makes her counter-offer ("Come with me . . ."), moving clockwise to west. The priest now moves clockwise, north to east, as he considers her offer ("Such a thing . . ."). He stops at east and steps through the ring of people into the center of the circle, offering his hand to the priestess ("If you will but . . ."). As the priestess accepts his proposal, she also steps inside the ring of people and takes his hand ("And I will show . . ."). They then hold hands above the altar, circling clockwise around it as they speak together ("Together we shall . . ."). Normally, all movement in a circle is *deosil*,[4] but I decided to have the priest and priestess move counter-clockwise during the first part of the chase-dance to symbolize that all was not right with the world.

After they came to center, the Priest and Priestess sat facing each other throughout the rest of the ritual, interacting with the audience only through the maiden. This was done to emphasize that the priest and priestess were playing the part of the God and Goddess, as well as

---

[4]Pronounced *jeh-shil*; usually translated as "sunwise," deosil literally means "southward" or "to the south," but the meaning is still the same: in summer the sun travels "to the south." The direction is what we call clockwise.

to symbolize the seclusion of the honeymoon. Also, when the priest and priestess shared the chalice, both held on to it while each of them drank. It was awkward, but effective.

VARIATIONS

As you can see, the staging of this ritual is highly intricate, and we had to rehearse it three or four times. The chase-dance worked very well, but you may wish to eliminate it to simplify the ritual. The text alone is enough to indicate what's going on. You may also want to have the priest and priestess interact with the audience directly instead of through a third party.

The second, most obvious variation is to make the ritual more interactive and have the audience be more involved. Adding invocations and having everyone sing the chants together is the simplest way to do this. You can also add a circle dance after all the candles are lit. You may also want to have some background music and more extensive decorations. The possibilities are really endless.

Chapter 7

Litha

Litha[1] is the longest day of the year, the day when the sun is at the height of its power. Many practices associated with May Day were also done at Litha, especially driving cattle through bonfires; in some areas the Maypole Dance was performed at this time. In Germany, the Lazy Man, a comic figure like Green George, goes about chasing the ladies and ringing a bell. People went into the woods to gather Saint-John's-Wort and mistletoe, bringing it back to their houses for protection.

Like Samhain, Litha is another day when the boundaries between the worlds are thin, when mortals had strange experiences, when fairies trooped across the land. This is because Litha is the intercalary or "extra" month of the Anglo-Saxon calendar, added every other year to bring the lunar months back in line with the solar year. Because of this, Litha is also a time of divination, particularly with "Diviner Eggs" and "Destiny Cakes." Each guest at a feast was given a small bowl and an egg. The egg was cracked into the bowl, and the guest would read his or her future in the shape. Destiny Cakes were small cakes baked into

---

[1]From the Anglo-Saxon, meaning "calm" or possibly "moon."

Figure 8. Litha.

various shapes and served under a cloth: each guest would reach under the cloth and pull out a cake, the shape of which foretold the future. Nervous lovers also had a special type of divination for Litha: they would bring a sprig of Saint-John's-Wort home and leave it out overnight. If the branch had not wilted in the morning, it indicated that their love would be long and strong.[2]

The nature of Litha as a "day outside of time" is vastly different from that of Samhain. There are no tales of ghosts or monsters loose at Midsummer, and the strange experiences one has are likely to be comic, harmless, or even beneficial. Litha has an "upside down" quality about it; that is, things often are reversed or mixed-up. A Midsummer's Eve riddle runs:

Green is Gold. (From new leaves, which are more golden than green.)

Fire's Wet.   (Candles are floated on water and wishes made on them.)

Future's Told. (This is a night of divination.)

Dragon's Met. (St. George kills a "dragon" in a Midsummer version of the Mummer's play.)[3]

Perhaps the best expression of the nature of Litha is found in Shakespeare's play *A Midsummer Night's Dream*, where four young lovers spend a very confusing night in the forest; the fairies are everywhere, interfering at every turn, and at the end no one is sure if it really happened or if it was only a dream.

Litha is also a night when the Wild Hunt is abroad, but it has none of the terrible aspects of the Hunt at Yule. This time, Woden or Herne rides his grey Cloud-Horse, riding across the sky so there will be plenty of rain for the growing season. This different aspect of the Wild

---

[2]Madeleine Pelner Cosman, *Medieval Holidays and Festivals: A Calendar of Celebrations* (New York: Charles Scribner's Sons, 1981), pp. 62, 63.

[3]Madeleine Pelner Cosman, *Medieval Holidays and Festivals*, pp. 57.

Hunt reflects the difference between a deadly winter storm and a pleasant summer storm.

The significance of Litha lies primarily in its paradoxes and contradictions. The biggest paradox is that of the solstice itself: even as the sun reaches the height of its power, it begins its decline, and the beginning of summer heralds the coming autumn and winter. The beginning of the sun's decline is symbolized by the rebirth of the Holly King, the Spirit of Winter. Even as the Oak King was reborn at Yule during the height of the Winter King's reign, the Holly King is reborn at Litha during the height of the Summer King's reign.

Litha Ritual

by Janice

Purpose: This ritual was designed to celebrate Litha as the festival of the Sun God at the height of his power. It is dedicated to the God in general and was written as a companion ritual to my Imbolg Ritual.

Decorations: The circle should be decorated with lots of greens and golds, and there should be oak branches on the altar. Some sort of sun symbol should be on the altar.

Necessary props: You will need three large candles on the altar: one gold, one green, and one dark brown. You will also need a glass bowl filled with a "Sun stone" such as citrine or amber, a wooden bowl filled with seeds, and a pottery bowl filled with fresh flowers and bones. The chalice should be gold or amber-colored, and filled with a golden wine or mead. You will also need a cauldron.

Number of people needed: Four—a priest or priestess, and three squires.

Costumes: One squire should be dressed as the Sun Lord—wearing gold with a sun symbol on a necklace and golden glitter scattered in his hair and on his shoulders. One is dressed as the Green Man—wearing green with a necklace made of acorns and a crown of oak leaves. The third is dressed as the Hunter—wearing dark brown with a necklace of horn or antler, carrying a sword and wearing an antlered headdress.

Background music: None.

THE RITUAL

Priest/Priestess: **This rite is held in honor of the God of Many Names and to witness the height of his power in his aspect as the Sun. I close this circle in his name and declare this sacred space.**

We would also give welcome to the Great Goddess who is his companion and our Lady of the Moon. May she join with us in this celebration of the God.

Invoke elements.

Priest/Priestess: **This is the festival of Midsummer. It is the longest day of the year, and one where the veils are once more thin between the realms of the Sidhe and the world of the mortal. It is a time for merriment and the making of wishes. On this day who knows what may happen and what may be granted?**

For this is the time sacred to the Solar King when he is at his strongest. He has reached the peak of his power and his rays shine out in glorious, golden splendor. His beauty and brilliance are such that none dare look at him for fear of being blinded by his light.

As everything in nature comes to its peak and then declines, so must the God in his aspect of the Sun. But that which declines is always transformed, and so it is with the God who takes on many aspects and wears many crowns.

Hear now the words of the God in his aspect of the Solar King.

Squire 1 (in gold) as the Sun Lord comes forth, holding the glass bowl of stones.

Sun Lord: **I am the fiery monarch of the Sun. I am the bringer of clarity. I am the Great Revealer and the Bestower of Enlightened Thought. I am the warmth that gently dries the rain from the Earth. I am the light that gilds the forest leaves with gold. I am the source of youthful love. From my enchanted harp comes the music of the heart. I am the Great Poet. I am the Eternal Lover. I am Apollo. I am Helios. I am Taliesin. I am Balder. I am he that sparks the seeds of the Earth to life.**

Squire 1 lights the gold candle. He then gives a stone to everyone present, saying:

Accept my gift. Accept the illumination of the sun.

Priest/Priestess: **Hear now the words of the God in his second aspect of the Green Man.**

Squire 2 (in green) as the Green Man steps forward, holding the wooden bowl of seeds.

Green Man: **I am the ancient Greenwood Lord. I am the Guardian of the Forest and all the creatures that dwell within it. I am crowned and bearded with verdant, twining greenery. I am rooted in the rich, brown earth. I am the soul of all things wild and I sing with the battle cry of the stag. My voice is the wind as it whispers and sighs through the tops of the trees. I am the strength of the oak. I am the mystery of nature, untamed and free. I am Pan. I am Faunus. I am Cernunnos. I am the Green Man. I am the ecstatic Player of the Pipes of life, and none can refuse to Dance the Wheel with me.**

Squire 2 lights the green candle. He then gives a seed to everyone present, saying:

Accept my gift. Accept the life of the land.

Priest/Priestess: **Hear now the words of the God in his aspect of the Hunter.**

Squire 3 (in brown) as the Hunter, steps forward carrying the pottery bowl filled with bones and flowers.

Hunter: **I am the Dark Guardian of the Gates of Death. I am the Leader of the Wild Hunt. I am Wind Rider and Storm Bringer. I am helmeted with steel and ice, crowned with horns of lightning. I am the Grey Master of the Winter sky. I am holder of** the keys to the hidden realms. I am the Soul of Midnight. I am the Lord of the Underworld. I ride the eight-legged sky-horse. I am Rune Master and Wisdom Keeper. I am the Riddle Maker. I am the Hunter. I am Hades. I am Woden. I am Gwynn ap Nudd. I am Herne. I am the Hunter who is one with the Hunted.

Squire 3 lights the brown candle. He then passes a flower and a bone to everyone present, saying:

Accept my gift. Accept the answer to the ancient riddle of death.

Everyone holds his or her gift from each aspect of the God in his or her left hand. The group joins hands, and the gifts are charged with energy while chanting:

Faunus, Anubis, Ganesha,
Cernnunos, Apollo, Woden,
Nuada.

The chant is continued while the Priest/Priestess lead the group in a circle dance. The dance is stopped, and the chalice is passed while the group sings:

We all come from the Sun God,
And to him we shall return,
Like a ray of sunshine
Streaming in the summer sky.

We all come from the Green Man,
And to him we shall return,
Like an acorn green
Falling to the forest floor.

We all come from the Hunter,
And to him we shall return,
Like a dove on white wings
Flying to its evening's rest.

Dismiss elements. Thank the Lord and Lady.

Priest/Priestess: **May the God protect you and guide you on your path. May the Goddess send you light and love. Our circle is open, but never broken. Merry meet, and merry part, and merry meet again!**

DIRECTIONS

The antlered or horned headdress can be made several ways. The one we use is a deerskin hood long enough to hang over the shoulders and down the back with a simple button-and-loop closure at the neck. We then stuck a small pair of antlers through the top of the hood. Small antlers are better; larger pairs can get very heavy on top of your head.

The key to getting the antlers to stand upright is to use a pair with the skull plate still intact. Place leather padding on the top and bottom of the skull plate and stitch it together. Then, cut small holes in the top of the hood and thread the antlers through. Stitch the leather surrounding the skull plate tightly to the inside of the hood. The double layer of leather gives it added support.

Other sorts of horns may be attached to a metal headband covered with leather to make it more comfortable. Raymond Buckland gives instructions on how to make horned headbands and helmets in his book, *Buckland's Complete Book of Witchcraft.*[4]

VARIATIONS

As in my Imbolg ritual, one person could play all three gods, but having three different people is very effective. The costuming can be reduced to very basic symbols of each aspect of the God, maybe even an appropriately colored sash. Songs and chants can be left out, or you can substitute your favorite ones instead. The circle dance can also be omitted.

---

[4]Raymond Buckland, *Buckland's Complete Book of Witchcraft* (St. Paul, MN: Llewellyn, 1986).

Chapter 8

Lammas

---- **August 1** ----

Lughnasadh   **Lughnassad**

As the name Lughnasadh[1] clearly suggests, this is the festival of the Celtic Sun God, Lugh, Lug, or Lleu Llaw Gyffes. The festival was held in Ireland at Tailltenn and in France at Lugundum (Lyons) to honor both Lugh and his foster-mother Tailltiu or Tailte. Games were held with the hope that the energy of the games would give strength to the Sun God, who brought fertility to the land. In some parts of Ireland, temporary or trial marriages, called "Tailltenn marriages," were contracted at this festival, and sometimes the king of Ireland was ritually married to a priestess who represented the goddess of the land.

Lughnasadh means "commemoration of Lugh." This is Lugh's wake; he has been betrayed by his wife, Blodeuwedd, and slain by her lover. Lugh, however, did not truly die—he was transformed into an eagle and later restored by his uncle, Gwydion. Lugh may be a later version of Bel, and his myth may represent either the cycle of the crops

---

[1]Pronounced *loo-nus-uh*; Lughnasadh is more properly the name of this festival, but Lammas has been in common usage since the 12th century. We use it here because it is much easier to spell and pronounce.

Figure 9. Lammas.

or more probably the cycle of the sun as it "dies" each autumn and returns to life in early spring. Lugh's wake brings in the first signs of autumn as the sun is killed.

In the agricultural cycle, Lammas is the harvest festival at which the Corn God is killed by the reapers. Traditionally, the last man to finish reaping was given the "Old Man" or "Old Hag," a corn doll representing the guilt of having killed the God. This doll had to be maintained as a person (fed, watered, and talked to) until Beltane of the following year, when it was burned in the new fire, and all guilt was cleansed. Harvest cakes were baked and offered as sacrifice at Lammas (the name comes from the Anglo-Saxon meaning "loaf-mass"), probably to commemorate the sacrificed Corn God. This is also the time, in some areas, when the Holly King defeats the Oak King in combat — with the death of the Oak King representing either the sacrifice of the Corn God or the end of summer that comes with the autumn harvest.

In both traditions of this festival, the common theme is the death of the God. It is also clear in both that the God is not gone forever; he will return in the cycle of the seasons. Even as his Lady is restored to youth and once again becomes the Maiden, the God is restored to life and once again becomes the King.

Lammas Ritual #1
by Janice

Purpose: The primary purpose of this ritual is to celebrate the harvest, commemorate the sacrifice of the Corn God, and to acknowledge the end of summer and the first stirrings of winter.

Decorations: Harvest fruits and vegetables: squash, gourds, wheat, corn, etc. Autumn colors — reds, browns, greens, and golds — should be used as much as possible. Use wood or clay candle holders and chalice.

Necessary props: You will need a basket filled with wheat, with small clay Goddess or "Venus" figures nestled in the wheat, a plate of harvest cakes or cookies, a large cauldron, and a chalice filled with dark red wine.

You will also need a hunting horn, a sword or large knife, any small sharp knife for the priestess, and a large piece of sheer black cloth (a large scarf or a piece of lightweight broadcloth).

Number of people needed: Six—one priest and two squires, and one priestess and two maidens.

Costumes: The priest wears a crown made of wheat or oak leaves. A green mantel or cloak and a horned headdress or a crown of holly leaves should be on the altar. (Warning: holly leaves are very sharp: if you want to use a holly crown, make sure your priest has a thick cloth to cover his head, and be very careful around his eyes!)

Background Music: None.

THE RITUAL

Invoke the elements. The Priest/Priestess invokes Bridget and Herne, saying:

Our Lady Bright, Bridget, Bri'id,
Reaper of the Corn King's seed;
Beloved of the Hornèd God,
You turn the Wheel as Arianrhod!

On moonlit heath and forests deep,
Or where your lady's willows weep,
Horn'd Cernunnos, Robin, Herne,
Be with us as the seasons turn!

Priestess: **This is the time of preparation, a time for sacrifice, a time of death. It is also a time of change, transformation, and rebirth. Now the Summer Goddess lays down her cloak of Greenery and takes up the dark mantel of the Crone. Now the King of the Grain is cut, harvested, and then reborn as the Lord of Winter, Grim Rider of the Wild Hunt, Keeper of the Gates of Death.**

The Priestess and the two Maidens echo the next lines off each other, with the Priestess speaking first, and the Maidens alternating.

Priestess: **I am the Summer Mother—**

Maiden 1: **Who will be the Dark Crone.**

Priestess: **I am the Green Earth—**

Maiden 2: **That soon will be bare.**

Priestess: **I am the First Fruits—**

Maiden 1: **That must dry for winter.**

Priestess: **I am the Giver of Life—**

Maiden 2: **Who deals the death blow.**

Priestess: **I am the Goddess—**

Maiden 1: **I am the Goddess—**

Maiden 2: **I am the Goddess.**

The Priest and two Squires alternate the following lines in the same way.

Priest: **I am the seed—**

Squire 1: **That was planted in spring.**

Priest: **I am the fire—**

Squire 2: **That brings forth life.**

Priest: **I am the grain—**

Squire 1: **That soon will be cut.**

Priest: **I am the Oak King—**

Squire 2: **Who soon must change crowns.**

Priest: **I am the God—**

Squire 1: **I am the God—**

Squire 2: **I am the God.**

Then the Priestess and Maidens begin again.

Priestess: **I am the love of the Greenwood Lord—**

Maiden 1: **He who will die by your hand.**

Priestess: **I am his death, the gentle slayer—**

Maiden 2: **She who will rebirth the slain.**

Then the Priest and Squires finish.

Priest: **I am the love of the Lady White—**

Squire 1: **She who shall strike you down.**

Priest: **I am the Summer Sacrifice—**

Squire 2: **He who shall be reborn.**

Priestess: **We are the balance of Life and Death.**

Priest: **We are the seasons of Light and Dark. Willingly do I give my body and blood for the reaping.**

The Priestess cuts the wheat crown from the head of the Priest, while the Maidens cover his head with a black cloth.

Priestess: **The Corn King is slain;
the Oak reign ends!**

The Priestess passes the plate of cakes, saying:

**Share the body of the Corn King
that His death may nourish our life.**

After the cakes are passed, the Priestess says:

**As the life of the Harvest Lord is given for the good of all, so is
he transformed and reborn for the good of all. The reign of the
Holly King shall begin as the Hunter is crowned!**

Maidens/Squires remove black cloth and dress the Priest in a green
mantle. They crown him with an antlered headdress while the Priestess
gives him a hunting horn and a sword. The Priestess passes basket of
statues, saying:

**Accept a gift of the Harvest Mother to keep as a promise of the
spring that will follow the winter.**

After the basket has gone around, the Priestess picks up the chalice,
saying:

**Bride, Lady of the Flaming Forge, keep the spark of life aglow
as we face the winter's cold. Prepare us for the spring that you
will bring again.**

**Herne, Horned Hunter, Greenwood Lord, let us grow within as
the Wheel does turn. Protect us well as the Wild Hunt rides!**

The chalice is passed while everyone sings "Lady Weave."[2] Dismiss elements. The Priest/Priestess thanks Bridget and Herne, saying:

---

[2]For complete text and music of songs, see Appendix A on page 111.

Herne, Guardian of the Gates,
Bride, Keeper of the Flame,
We thank you for joining our harvest rites.
Our circle is open: let the feasting begin!

Everyone leaves the circle singing "Merry Meet, Merry Part."

DIRECTIONS
The Goddess figurines we used were simple clay representations of a female figure, similar to the ancient "Venus" figurines. Any book on ancient myth or art will have pictures of these figures that you can use for examples. The most extensive study of these figures is Marija Gimbutas' *The Language of the Goddess*;[3] you are almost guaranteed to find a figure you like in here.

VARIATIONS
This ritual uses some elaborate costuming as part of its symbolism. If necessary, much of it could be eliminated or made simpler. Instead of the full set of props for the Holly King (sword, horn, green cloak, crown), you could use some simple symbol of the priest's role. One prop we recommend you keep is the black cloth to represent the death of the Oak King; it is a very simple symbol, and it is quite effective. Also, the number of people needed could be reduced if necessary, but you will need a minimum of one priestess and one priest.

The point of this ritual is to celebrate the sacrifice of the Corn God and the beginning of the reign of the Holly King; because of this, the Priest plays the major role. If this inequality is inappropriate, you could balance it somewhat by adding a costume for the priestess, perhaps emphasizing her role as slayer, and possibly having the priestess undergo a change of roles as well, most likely from Harvest Mother to Crone.

---

[3]Marija Gimbutas, *The Language of the Goddess: Unearthing the Hidden Symbols of Western Civilizations* (San Francisco: HarperCollins, 1991).

Lammas Ritual #2
by Veronica

Purpose: This ritual is dedicated to Lugh as his festival. It emphasizes the harvest aspect of the festival, especially the power of the Sun ripening the crops.

Decorations: General harvest symbols and colors—fruit, nuts, etc.—with an emphasis on golds and wheat. We also used a sun-face plaque as the centerpiece.

Necessary props: One large gold candle in the center of the altar. A plate of harvest cakes or cookies. A cauldron, and a chalice filled with mead or cider.

Number of people needed: We used two, but one will do.

Costumes: None.

Background Music: None.

THE RITUAL
Invoke elements.

Priest: **Lugh, shining Lord of the Sun, be with us as we celebrate your festival and work to bring the harvest in.**

Priestess: **Now is the time of shortening days and ripening fields. The long days of summer are past, and we watch our efforts come to fruition. All summer have we watched the shining sun and the gentle rain nourish the grain, and now it is time to gather in the harvest that we have worked for all summer.**

The Priest takes the golden candle and passes it to the person on his left, saying:

As the Sun ripens the growing fields, so will our own lives ripen and bear fruit. Place in this candle anything in your life that you wish to come to fruition.

Each person meditates on the candle for a few minutes, then passes it to the next person; when everyone is finished, the Priest takes the candle and places it back at the center of the altar. He lights the candle, saying:

Lugh, Lord of the Sun, let your power burn in our lives as your fire burns in this candle, and let all we desire come to pass.

The group holds hands and starts a circle dance, while the Priest and Priestess begin the chant:

All: **Gold, gold the candle burns.**
Gold, gold the wheatfield turns.

Priestess: **Golden glows the northern star.**
Golden ripe the apples are.
Golden is the small wheat seed.
Let the fire address our need.

All: **Gold, gold the candle burns.**
Gold, gold the wheatfield turns.

Priest: **Golden does the new day dawn.**
Golden is the Lady's song.
Golden turns the grassy field.
Greatly let our efforts yield.

All: **Gold, gold the candle burns.**
Gold, gold the wheatfield turns.

Priest: **Golden shines the Sun at noon.**
Golden glows the harvest Moon.
Golden burns the cauldron's fire.
Now let ripen our desire.

All: **Gold, gold the candle burns.**
Gold, gold the wheatfield turns.

Priestess: **Golden grows the western sky.**
Golden shines the black cat's eye.
Golden seas adorn the west.
Now the fruit is at its best.

All: **Gold, gold the candle burns.**
Gold, gold the wheatfield turns.

Priest: **Golden does the candle shine.**
Let us bring the harvest in.

All: **Gold, gold the candle burns.**
Gold, gold the wheatfield turns.

Priestess: **Golden straws become the broom.**
Let us take the harvest home.

All: **Gold, gold the candle burns.**
Gold, gold the wheatfield turns.

The dance stops. The Priest blows out the candle, saying:

It is done. The harvest comes to us. Take this symbol of the harvest and remember that all things come to fruition.

The Priest passes the plate of cakes while the group sings:

Nature is a Wheel—
Life has no end.
When the cycle is complete,
We begin again.

Priestess: **Let us thank Lugh as we bring the harvest in.**

The Priestess passes the chalice.

Dismiss the elements.

Priest: **Lugh, shining one, Lord of the Sun, we bid you goodbye as the winter comes.**

Priestess: **The harvest is in! Let the feasting begin!**

The group leaves the circle singing "Merry Meet, Merry Part."

VARIATIONS
Although we used two people to do this ritual, the number of people involved could vary from one to four, with each person taking a different verse of the chant, and men or women could read any part you wish. You could give everyone a small candle instead of using the large single one; if you do this, you may still want to have a large one at the center for effect.

If you want to make the ritual more theatrical, you can add costumes and background music, or increase the number of people reading the verses of the chant. If you want to make the ritual more simple, the dance could be left out, as could the plate of cakes and the songs.

Chapter 9

Autumn Equinox

——— September 23 ———

Michaelmas　　　**Mabon**　　　**Modron**

Most of the tradition surrounding this holiday has been lost. The Anglo-Saxon name for the month of September, *halegmonath* or *holy month*, indicates that they held it in special significance, but we do not know exactly why. We do know that this festival celebrates the completion of the harvest and the beginning of preparations for winter. This is the day when farmers settled their accounts, paying their rent and other debts to the landowners. It is also a time of rest, of recuperating from the hard work of the harvest before winter arrives.

Michaelmas, or St. Michael's Day (September 29), has long been a popular festival in Britain, and it is possible that the earlier Anglo-Saxon festival was absorbed so early that no one remembers its original name or significance. St. Michael, one of the archangels of the Christian tradition, is most known for his victorious battle against the forces of evil that restored order to the cosmos. Michael is also known as a protector and healer and was often appealed to by those suffering from illness or injustice.

We have not found the original source for calling this festival *Mabon* or *Modron*; in fact, it seems to have originated sometime in the 20th century. Mabon is the name of an early Celtic deity about whom little

Figure 10. Mabon.

information is available. Mabon or Maponus was worshipped as the Divine Youth in both Gaul and Britain, and the Romans identified Maponus with Apollo as a god of music and youth, possibly hunting and the sun as well. Modron is the name of Mabon's mother, and it seems she is one of the Great Mother goddesses. Both Mabon and Modron are titles, meaning Son and Mother. Mabon appears in the Welsh tale "Culhwch and Olwen"[1] as the Great Prisoner, taken from his mother when he was three days old and held captive at Gloucester. The reason for his imprisonment is unknown, but it seems that this holiday may celebrate his release and reunion with his mother.

Although there is little information available about this holiday, the information that we do have shows a common theme: that of rebalancing or setting things right. The day of settling debts, the time of rest after the harvest, the feast of the healer and bringer of justice, and the release of the prisoner all fit the idea of the equinox as a time of balance, of rectifying the situation. This concept is strengthened by the fact that the Autumn Equinox falls on the cusp of Libra, the Sign of the Balance. Things must be set back into balance before the winter comes, or nothing will survive.

Autumn Equinox Ritual
by Veronica

Purpose: This ritual concentrates on the equinox as a time of almost violent rebalancing, when the autumn storms come to restore the earth after the harvest. For this reason, I dedicated the ritual to Mannanan Mac Ler or Manawydan ab Llyr; Mannanan is the Irish storm god and wields the lightning sword that answers all wrongs. His wife Rhiannon, a goddess of horses and of fertility, is especially known for her endurance and strength.

Decorations: I used a sword as the symbol for the God, and a statue of a horse for the Goddess.

---

[1]Found in the *Red Book of Hergest*, commonly referred to in English as *The Mabinogion*. Available in translation by Jeffrey Gantz. (London: Penguin Books, 1976).

Necessary props: Chalice and cauldron.
Number of people needed: Two—one Priest and one Priestess.
Costumes: None.
Background Music: A "Sounds of Nature" tape of a thunderstorm.

THE RITUAL
Invoke elements:

Earth: **Spirits of Earth, breathlessly awaiting the rejuvenating storm, lend us your strength that we may endure the pain of growth.**

Air: **Spirits of Air, wind-heralds of the storm, fill the sails of our minds and carry us gently to the wisdom of the sky.**

Fire: **Spirits of Fire, who dance as lightning through the sky, shed your light upon our lives and guide us along our way.**

Water: **Spirits of Water, gather in the clouds and return to the Earth as rain. Bring us your cool, refreshing streams and wash away all doubt and fear.**

The Priest/Priestess invokes Mannanan and Rhiannon, saying:

Mannanan, son of the sea and lord of the storm, all the Earth stands in awe of your power. Draw your sword and set everything aright once more.

Rhiannon, blessed lady of the horses, stand with us through the storm. Grant us your courage and endurance while your lord restores the balance of the world.

Priest: **The grass begins to shrink in the power of the Sun.**
Small streams that were once mighty rivers
dry,
and leave the dying Earth

Cracked and parched.
And off in the west, between the Moon and the sea,
I begin to stir.

Priestess: The cycle of the Sun is over. The Earth is dry and old.
Mannanan rides from the seas once more and bids farewell to
his brother-sun. His Cloud Horse's hoofbeats echo the thunder-
rhythm—drawing the winds in his track.

Priest: My Lady Earth cries out in the relentless sun,
And my children fade and die.
Their blood flows to Heaven, to Me,
Fueling my power and feeding my rage.
I summon forth the elements—
Wind and water, dust and lightning—
And bind them to myself.
Their power is mine, is Me,
And I am born.

Priestess: Mannanan sweeps the sky, sword in hand, and lightning flashes every stroke. The balance must be restored. The
sky lets flow its tears, and life flows back to the Earth.

Priest: I scream, and weep bitterly
As white-fire knives rend me in two.
Pain infuriates me,
And I vent my rage against the Earth,
Tearing the trees and pounding flowers
Into colorful corpses.
All things cower in the face of my fury.
I am Power.
I reign supreme.

Priestess: The Earth, tired and drained from the birth and the
harvest, gratefully accepts the restoration of the rain. She ab-
sorbs the water and the power and prepares for her winter rest.

Priest: **The Earth, meanwhile, endures me, humors me,**
Until my wrath is spent.
While I gasp out my life,
She smiles a pregnant smile.
Already my children lie fallow in her womb,
And for all the destruction and death,
The stagnant smell is the scent of Life.
Those who know me understand,
And see beauty even in dead flowers.

Priestess: **Now Mannanan, son of the sea and lord of the sky, lays**
aside his Lightning Sword and gently takes his Lady's hand.
Now the Storm is spent, its power distributed to all things, re-
newing them. The new world shines in the full Moon—washed
clean and dripping with rainbows.

Priest/Priestess takes up chalice saying:

May the power of Mannanan help us find the balance within,
and the strength of Rhiannon help us endure the painful times.

The Priestess passes the chalice while the group sings:

Blow, Winds! Winds, blow!
Rain will come, and pain will go.
Flash of Lightning, guide the lost ones
Through the Storm.

Dismiss elements. Thank Mannanan and Rhiannon. Close the circle.

VARIATIONS
Having two people read the ritual works best; that way, one reads the
poem, and the other reads the explanation. However, one person could
read the ritual if necessary; if this is done, I recommend that the reader
pause between the "priest" and "priestess" parts, making certain that
the audience is aware of the change of speaker.

This is mainly a performance ritual; if you'd like to have your audience more involved, you could add some type of chant or refrain between the priest and priestess parts. As a very simple chant, "Mannanan! Rhiannon!" has a nice rhythm, and it rhymes. Also, you could have some sort of storm symbol in the circle. After reading the text, pass the storm symbols and let each member of the group choose one; then charge the symbols with energy, asking Mannanan and Rhiannon to help your group endure the necessary pain of restoring balance in their lives.

Songs and Chants

Merry Meet, Merry Part

(Words and music by Leuwyn of the Silver Wheel Coven)

Mer-ry do we meet and mer - ry part

Peace in our souls joy in our hearts.

Cir - cle is bro - ken feast-ing can be - gin.

Mer-ry do we part, to meet a - gain.

Merry do we meet, and merry part,
Peace in our souls, joy in our hearts.
Circle is broken; feasting can begin.
Merry do we part, to meet again.

LADY WEAVE (VARIATIONS)
(Verses adapted by Veronica)

Master, lead your Hunt tonight
Bathed in your Lady's silver light.
Earth and Air and Fire and Water
Ride in your train.

Blow, Winds; Winds, blow!
Rain will come and pain will go.
Flash of Lightening, guide the lost ones
Through the storm.

(Original words and music are from an old traditional English round titled "Rose.")

Rose, Rose, Rose, Rose,
Will I ever see thee wed?
I will marry at thy will, Sire,
At thy will.

Lady Weave

(Original words by Finn of the Covenstead of Eleu)

Lady weave your circle tight.
Spin a web of glowing light.
Earth and Air and Fire and Water
Bind us to Her.

Invocation

(Words and music by Shara of Flaming Arc Coven)

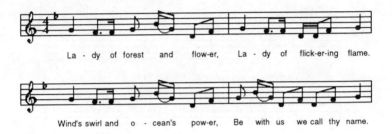

Lady of forest and flower,
Lady of flickering flame.
Wind's swirl and ocean's power,
Be with us we call thy name.

INVOCATION (VARIATIONS)
(Verse adapted by Janice)

Lord Herne of forest and bower,
Brigid of flickering flame.
The Dance calls with love and power
Join with us, we call your name.

(Verse adapted by Veronica)

Brigid of shining fire,
Lady of flickering flame.
Grant us our hearts' desire,
Be with us, we call your name.

The Goddess Chant
(Original words by Deena Metzger)

Isis, Astarte, Diana,
Hecate, Demeter, Kai,
Inanna.

GOD CHANT
(Adapted by Janice)

Faunus, Anubis, Ganesha,
Cernunnos, Apollo, Woden, Nuada!

OSTARA DYING AND RISING GOD CHANT
(Adapted by Veronica)

Tammuz, Adonis, Dumuzi,
Dionysus, Attis, Pelles,
Osiris.

From the Goddess

We all come from the Goddess
And to her we shall return.
Like a drop of rain
Flowing to the ocean.

FROM THE GOD
(Adapted by Janice)

We all come from the Sun God,
And to him we shall return.
Like a ray of sunshine,
Streaming in the summer sky.

We all come from the Green Man,
And to him we shall return.
Like an acorn green,
Falling to the forest floor.

We all come from the Hunter,
And to him we shall return.
Like a dove on white wings,
Flying to its evening's rest.

IMBOLG VARIANT
(Adapted by Veronica)

We all come from the Maiden
And to her we shall return
Like the budding flowers
Blooming in the springtime.

We all come from the Mother
And to her we shall return
Like a grain of wheat
Falling to the reaper's scythe.

We all come from the Wise One
And to her we shall return
Like the waning moon
Shining on the winter snow.

OSTARA DYING AND RISING GOD VARIANT
(Adapted by Veronica)

Isis waits for Osiris
Inanna for Tammuz
Aphrodite for Adonis
Waiting for her love's return.

The Lady waits for her lover
To return from the Western World
Now the sun grows strong
And the waters flow again.

The Lady waits for her lover
To return from the Western World
Now the warm sun calls
And the world comes back to life.

The Lady waits for her lover
To return from the Western World
Now the gates swing wide
And the earth rejoices.

For the music to the "Goddess Chant" and "From the Goddess" (also used for the adaptations) see the tape "From the Goddess" by On the Wings of Song and Robert Gass listed in the Resources section.

Nature is a Wheel

(Words by Gwydion of the Silver Wheel Coven, sung to the tune of "Row, Row, Row Your Boat")

Nature is a Wheel;
Life has no end.
When the cycle is complete,
We begin again.

Appendix B

Circle Dances

The most simple version of a circle dance is to walk around the circle. For example, in Janice's Yule ritual, we put our hands into the circle to form the spokes of the wheel, then simply turned and walked around the circle. In Janice's Beltane ritual, we all held onto cords—the men forming one line led by the Priest and the women forming another line led by the Priestess. The men walked around the circle counterclockwise while the women walked clockwise, weaving in and out like the child's game of "Bluebird" or "In and Out the Window." You can hold hands while doing this if your circle is small enough, but if you try to go too fast, you could trip.

Another simple circle dance, one that's easier to do while holding hands, is to step sideways around the circle. Just take a side step with your left foot, then bring your right foot over to close with your left. This "step, close" pattern is the basic step of most circle dances; simply repeat this step in time to the music or chant, stepping with your left foot on the down beat and closing with your right foot on the up beat. Since your feet never have to cross each other, the danger of anyone tripping is very small.

This circle dance can be varied in a number of ways. A simple medieval dance uses the "step, close" pattern, moving three steps to the left, one step back to the right, three to the left, one to the right, and so on. For faster, more energetic dances, stomp the floor with your right foot as you close, making the pattern "step, stomp." It's a lot of fun!

The chant we used in our Ostara ritual has an uneven number of beats in the last line, making it difficult to dance to. Our solution was to take the "step, close" pattern, then stand in place and clap hands on the last line, as follows:

TAM- muz, a-	DON- is, du-	MUZ- i,
step close	step close	step close
DI- o-ny-sus,	AT- tis,	PEL- les,
step close	step close	step close
	o- SIR- is	
	(stand in place) clap clap	

Notice that not every syllable has a beat and some of the syllables run together. Only take steps on the accented syllables. The rests at the beginning and the end of the last line gave us a chance to drop hands to clap and then join hands again. It took a little practice; we did it once or twice through before we did the ritual.

At Beltane and Samhain, we usually get together all day for games and dancing. We usually do various medieval and English country dances, such as "Gathering Peascods," "Half Han'agan," "the Horse Bransle," "Icka-Nicka," and "the Maltese Bransle." These folk dances are too complicated to go into here, but information on them should be available in your local library under "Folk Dances — English," "Country Dances," or "Medieval Dances." If you have a folk dancing or medieval re-creation group in your area, they should be able to help you find sources for country dances. Also, many renaissance fairs have a dance troupe that you might be able to ask.

The Maypole Dance

The basic idea of the Maypole is to take ribbons and weave them around a pole. Most often you will see the pole wrapped a single time; when I learned the Maypole Dance for a performance at a renaissance fair, we wrapped and unwrapped the pole several times before we finally tied it off. The directions here are the way that I learned the dance; you can take or leave any of the steps and end the dance whenever you wish.

A few notes on "terminology:" The Maypole Dances ideally should have an even number of couples, usually eight (a total of sixteen people). The men and women alternate in the circle; the woman at the man's left is considered his partner. One couple is designated as lead or head couple; this couple decides when to stop the rounds, when to reverse direction, etc. The other dancers follow the head couple's lead.

If you don't have these exact arrangements, the dance will still work, but for ease of reference, I will assume the ideal arrangement: male, female, male, female, in an equal number of couples.

The Gathering Dance

Most often, the Maypole will begin with a Gathering Dance. The dancers are arranged in a very wide circle around the pole. As the music starts, the dancers skip in toward the pole until their circle becomes small enough that they can hold hands. They join hands and dance around in a circle once, until each dancer comes back (approximately) to his or her starting position. They drop hands and do a single arm turn with their partner on the right hand, turn and do a single arm turn on the left hand (the "swing your partner" step of a square dance). They reform the circle and skip four steps in towards the center, then four back to their places. The men walk forward and pick up two ribbons side by side, then walk back and hand the extra ribbon to their partner. The dancers step away from the pole until the ribbons are taut. For a simpler version of the Gathering Dance, the dancers may skip in towards the pole until they can hold hands, dance a single circle clockwise around the pole, and then go and get their ribbons.

The Candy Stripe

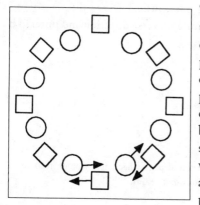

The women take one or two steps toward the pole; the men take one or two steps away from the pole. The women then dance counterclockwise around the pole, going around the circle once. When the women come back to their starting place, they stop; the men then dance clockwise around the pole, going around the circle once and stopping when they reach their starting place. The dance continues in this way, first women then men, either through a set number of rounds, usually three or six, or until the head couple decides the ribbons are too short to duck under easily. (If you have alternating colors of ribbons, the wrapped pole will look like a striped candy cane, hence the name.)

When the pole is wrapped, the dancers reverse direction and unwrap the pole. The men go first this time, dancing counterclockwise, and then the women dance clockwise. (The pattern is the same as the Reverse Candy Stripe described next.) The dance continues this way until the pole is unwrapped.

The Reverse Candy Stripe

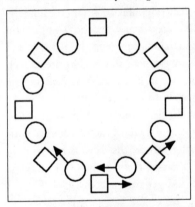

After the Candy Stripe is unwrapped, you can simply continue the unwrapping pattern and wrap the pole again; the pattern is the same as unwrapping the Candy Stripe. This time, the men will go first, counterclockwise, and then the women dance clockwise. In the version I learned, the women still stayed in towards the pole;[1] however, if you wish, you can have the men and women trade places for the Reverse Candy Stripe, the men coming in towards the pole and the women stepping out a little.

When the pole is wrapped, simply reverse direction and unwrap it (i.e., do the "regular" Candy Stripe).

---

[1]Having the women closer to the pole evolved out of necessity: women tend to be shorter than men and get under the ribbons more easily.

The Single Weave

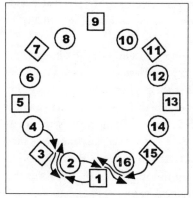

This is the most common form of the Maypole Dance; most people will simply do the Single Weave once and stop. Unwrapping the weaves does take a bit of practice; if any dancer has made a mistake in the wrapping, the unwrapping will be tricky. If, however, you don't unwrap the pole, any mistakes in the wrap are unimportant.

Again, the women take one step toward the pole, the men take one step away. The dancers turn to face their partner (men turn to the left, women to the right), then begin to dance, the men going clockwise and the women counterclockwise. This time, however, the dancers will weave in and out, men going "over" their partner, then "under" the next woman, and so on. Women will go under their partner, then over the next man, and so on.

If you start with an even number of couples, you will simply repeat the first round over and over again, always going over and under the same people—that is, dancer #1 will always go over dancer #2, under #4, over #6, under #8, etc. With an odd number of couples, the dancers will end up alternating, one round going over their partner, the next round going under, and so on. An even number of couples makes the dance much easier.

When the ribbons begin to get too short, the head couple calls "Last round." The dancers continue the round, stopping when they are facing their partners once again. The dancers then reverse direction and unwrap the pole. Now the men will go counterclockwise, still starting *over* their partners; the women will go clockwise, starting *under* their partners. Anyone you went under on the wrap you will still go under on the unwrapping. (This is about the same pattern as the Reverse Single Weave shown on page 124.)

Unwrapping the pole isn't as difficult as it sounds. If you get confused or you think you made a mistake on the wrap, you can simply *watch your ribbon at the top of the pole.* If your ribbon is under the ribbon of the person you're passing, then you have to go under that person now; it's as easy as that. The biggest trick is not bumping into anyone while you're watching your ribbon!

The Single Weave is very easy once you get into the pattern: over one, under the next; if you went over the last person you have to go under the next person. Once you get the rhythm down, it's very simple; you really only have to remember whether you went over or under the last person you passed. Another thing to remember is to simply keep going if you make a mistake. As I said earlier, mistakes only matter if you unwrap the pole, and not very much even then. Once you understand how to wrap and unwrap the Single Weave, you'll see that the other dances follow the exact same pattern.

The Reverse Single Weave

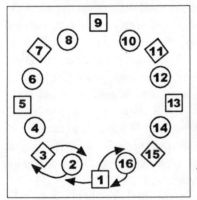

You guessed it. This is just the Single Weave starting in the opposite direction, the same pattern as unwrapping the Single Weave except with the women going *over* first, clockwise and the men *under* first, going counterclockwise. If you've done the Single Weave and are unwrapping it, just keep dancing when the pole is unwrapped and you're doing the Reverse Single Weave: unwrapping the Single Weave and wrapping the Reverse Single Weave are the same thing. When the pole is wrapped, reverse direction and unwrap it (just like you were wrapping the Single Weave).

The Double Weave (Couple's Weave)

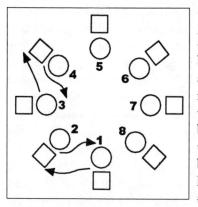

After the pole is unwrapped, the partners face the pole and pair off—joining hands, linking elbows, or holding each other around the waist, whichever is most comfortable. The couple will hold both of the partner's ribbons; this is easiest if you place the ribbons together and have both partners hold on with one hand. The head couple (couple #1) then turn to their left; the couple to their left (couple #2) turn to face them, and the others follow suit—"odd" couples turning left and "even" couples turning right.

The couples then begin to dance in the same pattern as in the Single Weave, "odd" couples going over first, clockwise; "even" couples going under, counterclockwise, in the same pattern as the Single Weave.

When the head couple decides the ribbons are getting too short, they call "Last round." As in the Single Weave, the dancers continue until each couple is facing their original "partner." The dancers then reverse direction and unwrap the pole. The unwrapping pattern is about the same as the Reverse Double Weave, described next.

The Reverse Double Weave

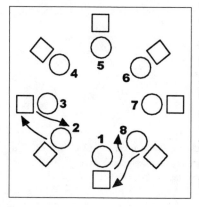

This dance is simply the Double Weave starting in the opposite direction. Again, if you have done the Double Weave and are unwrapping it, continue dancing after the pole is unwrapped to start the Reverse Double Weave.

Generally, the Reverse Double Weave is the final dance, and the pole is tied off instead of unwrapped.

After you have finished the last dance (whichever one you want to stop with), the pole is tied off with a Tying-Off Dance. The dancers continue until they can no longer get under the ribbons. Then they stop and hand their ribbons to the man in the head couple, the May King, or whoever else has been designated to tie off the pole. The head man gathers all the ribbons into a single handful, then wraps them once around the pole and pulls the end through (tying a half hitch, the first half of a bow or square knot). The dancers then rejoin hands and back away from the pole, forming their original circle again. Then, the dancers may do the Gathering Dance in reverse, starting with four steps in towards the pole and four steps out. Drop hands and do a single arm turn on the left hand, then a single arm turn on the right hand. The dancers then reform the circle and dance once around the pole clockwise, then drop hands and back away.[2] If you used the simpler Gathering Dance, you'll want to use the simpler Tying Off Dance, and vice versa.

---

[2]Traditionally, they would drop hands and run, the men chasing their partners, winning a kiss if they caught them before they passed a designated point. If you want to keep up this tradition, you may warn your dancers beforehand!

Deity and Element Symbols

God and Goddess Symbols: For ease of reference, we divide the many aspects of the Goddess into three major archetypes (Maiden/Mother/Crone) and the many aspects of the God into Sun/Vegetation/Horned God archetypes. This division is a generalization of the various attributes of the God and Goddess—many deities will share attributes of more than one archetype, and some will not fit at all. When deities have more than one attribute, we have listed them under their minor or secondary attribute in parentheses. The symbols are some basic suggestions: use any symbol that you feel is appropriate.

MAIDEN

Artemis, Blodeuwedd, Bri'id, Eos, Eostre, Diana, Freya, Kore.

The Maiden is the Bringer of Spring, the Lady of Flowers, the Virgin Huntress, Goddess of the Waxing Moon. She is associated with youth, dawn, inspiration, new beginnings, healing, and freedom. Her colors are white and silver, and her symbols are flowers, crescents, arrows, clear crystals, fire, and owl's or dove's feathers.

MOTHER

Aphrodite, Arianrhod, Cerridwen, Danu, Demeter, Inanna, Ishtar, Isis, Modron, Rhiannon, Tailltiu.

The Mother is both the fertile Earth and the Queen of Heaven, the Bringer of the Ripe Harvest. She gives birth to all life, including her lover/son who is the Dying and Rising God. She is the earliest form of

Figure 11. Venus.

the Goddess worshipped on Earth and is associated with growth, fulfillment, prosperity, sexuality, the full moon, maturity, love, and sovereignty. Her color is red; her symbols are harvest fruits, wheat, cauldrons, chalices, cow horns, bread, and bright-colored stones.

CRONE

(Arianrhod), Cailleach, (Cerridwen), Hecate, Kali, Morrigan, Persephone.

The Crone is the Wise Woman, Bringer of Death, Grandmother of Time, Keeper of Knowledge, and Asker of Riddles. She takes the soul through the gates of death and brings it back to rebirth. She is darkness and winter, the dark of the moon. She is associated with wisdom, divination, prophecy, endings, old age, rest, and secrets. Her color is black, and her symbols are raven's feathers, bones, spirals, broomsticks, and dark-colored stones.

SUN GODS

Apollo, Balder, Belenus, Helios, Mabon, Lleu, Mithras, Taliesin.

The Sun God is more generally the God of light, beauty, youth, music, healing, and the arts. The Sun God is always young, handsome, and well-loved. His colors are red and gold, and his symbols are fire, sun-faces, eagle's or hawk's feathers, and yellow stones.

VEGETATION GODS

Adonis, Attis, Dionysus, Dumuzi, (Lleu), Osiris, Pelles, Tammuz.

The Vegetation God is the Spirit of the Crops, the Dying and Rising God, Beloved of the Great Mother. He is the grain that is sacrificed for the good of the people. When he is gone from the earth, the Goddess goes into mourning, and the whole earth is barren. His colors are green and brown, and his symbols are wheat, corn, flowers (especially dark-colored), seeds, and phallic symbols.

HORNED GODS

Cernnunos, (Faunus), Gwynn ap Nudd, (Hades), Herne, Odin, (Pan), Woden.

The Horned God is the Wild Man of the Woods, the Master of the Animals. He was originally a God of hunting and is the oldest known aspect of the God. He is Lord of the Forests and Master of the Greenwood, the incarnation of the power and vigor of untamed nature. He is also called "Lord of the Dance" and is the most popular aspect of the God among Wiccans. The Horned God also has connections with death and the Underworld; as a hunting God, the stag-headed Horned God is both the predator and the prey. The Horned God leads the spirits of the dead on the Wild Hunt, and he is often considered the Keeper of the Gates of Life and Death. As ruler of the Underworld, the Horned God is also the keeper of the great treasures of the Earth. His colors are dark green and black, and his symbols are antlers, oak leaves, holly leaves, knives, swords, arrows, and coins.

Symbols and Herbs for the Elements: Next to the altar, the elemental points in a circle receive the most attention and detail when decorating. The element points mark the four directions — north (earth), east (air), south (fire), and west (water) — and the symbols represent the forces that govern each. In most circles, there will be a candle, some sort of symbolic representation of the element, and herbs to be used as a gift to the spirits of that element. After the element is invoked and the candle has been lit, the herbs are always placed in the cauldron. Also usually present are a container of salt at earth, incense at air, an extra candle at fire, and a shell containing water at water.

Each element has certain colors, gemstones, and animals associated with it. These come from many different cultures but often are very similiar for the element in question. Each also has certain herbs that are associated with it. Often these are obvious. Hot, fiery herbs like cayenne pepper, cinnamon, and cloves are associated with fire. Mosses and kelp are for water, and light, floating ferns represent the element of air. Sometimes the comparisons are not so obvious but usually it's easy to find the right herb for an element just by thinking about what the element represents. Some herbs are associated with more than one element. Use herbs in the way that feels right for you.

A good guide is to learn what each element stands for and then look at your herbs, stones, and animals. Earth is connected to the material things in our world, to birth and death, and is considered a place of great power and mystery. Air rules over all forms of communication and mental pursuits and deals with creativity, ideas, and knowledge. Fire holds the passion of love and represents life and energy. It can also be used for protection. Water is the flow of the emotions and represents the unconscious, feelings, intuition, and love. Choosing symbols that you feel an affinity for will make it that much easier to connect with the different elements and bring them into your ritual. (See figure 12 on page 132 for example setups for each elemental point.)

EARTH

Herbs: birch, cypress, grains (oats, wheat, barley, corn, rye), honeysuckle, mugwort, patchouli, sorrel, vervain, vetivert, yellowdock.

Symbols: dark stones, hematite, crystals, stones, iron, pewter, lead, fields, trees, pentacles, fruit, coins, caves, cattle, cow horns, night, winter, ice, snow, black, brown, dark green.

AIR

Herbs: almond (all nut trees), acacia, broom, clover, dandelion, lavender, maple, mint, mistletoe, pine, sage, star anise.

Symbols: amethyst, clear crystals, lapis, blades, scales, winds, high mountains, clouds, falling leaves, storms, bows, crescent moons, feathers, birds, antlers, light blue, white, silver, purple, spring, dawn.

Figure 12. Fire element (top left); Water element (top right); Earth element (bottom left); Air element (bottom right).

FIRE

Herbs: allspice, bay, cedar, cinnamon, citrus, clove, copal, dragon's blood, frankincense, garlic, ginger, holly, juniper, mullein, nutmeg, oak, rosemary, rowan, sandalwood, tobacco, wormwood.

Symbols: citrine, jasper, gold, brass, bronze, rods, staves, candles, horses, dragons, salamanders, deserts, sun, summer, noon, phallic symbols, red, orange, yellow, ram's horns.

WATER

Herbs: aloe, apple (all fruit trees), chamomile, coltsfoot, columbine, comfrey, eucalyptus, heather, iris/orris, jasmine, lilac, lotus, moonwort, myrrh, myrtle, thyme, violet, willow, yarrow.

Symbols: moonstone, "milky" stones, sea pebbles, holed stones, silver, cups, cauldrons, lakes, rivers, streams, ocean, driftwood, shells, seaweed, coral, mirrors, autumn, twilight, dark blue, light green.

Games

Here are a few of the games we like to play at holidays; there are countless others.

SAMHAIN
We play a lot of traditional Hallowe'en games at Samhain. (They were originally Samhain Games, anyway!) We have a costume contest, bob for apples, "pin the _____ on the _____." (We will usually pin the broom on the witch, the eyes on the jack-o'-lantern, the tail on the cat, or anything else appropriate.) We also do a variant of bobbing for apples where the apple is tied to a string and suspended from the ceiling. Participants then must hold their hands behind their back and attempt to bite the apple.

Samhain is also a good time for divining. We often do actual readings for each other with cards, runes, or whatever method; we also like to play some simple divining games. "Pick the odd card" is very easy and lots of fun. Place two red cards and one black card facedown on the table and mix them up. The game is to see who can find the odd card the most number of times. We often use a crystal or needle on a string as a pendulum to help us guess the card. Another variant of the card game pairs people up as teams. One person picks a card; the other person tries to guess the card while the first person says only if the number or suit is correct. The team with the least number of guesses to get the correct answer wins.

"Find your apple" works better with a more experienced group. Everyone is given an apple and marks it in some way. Each person spends a few moments holding the apple, getting the "feel" of it. Then, blindfold each person and put three apples in front of each of them. The game is to pick your own apple from the three without actually touching the apples.

Another game for an experienced group is "stone guessing." Everyone blindly picks a stone from a dish. They hold the stone for a few minutes, seeing what kind of impressions they get from it. These impressions could be color, heat, coolness, pictures, anything. Then, everyone looks at the stone to see what it is and looks up the magical properties of the stone to see if their impressions fit the stone. Often, we give everyone the same kind of stone when we play this. It's amazing how many people get the same impressions from the stones.

BELTANE

Our primary form of entertainment at Beltane is dancing, particularly dancing the Maypole. For instructions on the Maypole Dance, see Appendix B. We also make wreaths of flowers for everyone to wear; instructions for this are included after Janice's Beltane Ritual.

Other games we play are for choosing the May King and Queen. Usually, we choose the May Queen by taking a cupcake for each woman present and sticking some little prize (a crystal or something) inside one of them. Whoever gets the cupcake with the prize is the May Queen. The same method can be used to choose the May King, but we will more often use "Sticking the Straw Man."

"Sticking the Straw Man" is very similar to a piñata. We form a man out of straw or grass. Simply make a two- to three-foot wooden frame in the shape of a stick-man and tie straw around it with twine. The straw should be fairly thick, about six or eight inches around the "body." The straw man is suspended from the roof or a tree. (This game is messy; do it outdoors if possible.) The men are blindfolded and handed a stick or a sword; one by one they try to stab the straw man. The first one to stab the straw man is crowned the May King. After the May King is crowned, the straw man is torn apart and part of it burned in the Beltane fire.

Another game we always do is "Blindfolded Drawing." The group picks something to draw, ideally something that is somewhat familiar to everyone. Our group always draws pigs; everyone has some idea what a pig looks like, but no one has any experience drawing them. Also, the results are usually very funny. Each person is blindfolded, handed a pen or pencil, and pointed at an easel or piece of paper pinned to the wall. Then each person tries to draw. We award prizes for the best drawing, the funniest drawing, or anything else that strikes us. (One year we awarded a prize for "Best Moose" in our pig-drawing contest.)

Another game we play (outside!) if weather permits is "Green George." One man volunteers to be Green George; he has to be picked in advance so he can bring a bathing suit. We take all the extra strands of ivy from the wreaths and tie them around Green George, being careful not to restrict his arms or legs. Then buckets of water are placed in strategic locations around the yard and everyone except George is given a cup. The game is essentially a water fight—everyone versus George. Although George starts out with no cup, he can use his hands to throw water, pick up any cup that is dropped, or even pick up the entire bucket when it gets light enough.

Although George takes the brunt of the water, everybody gets at least a little wet during this game. It's a good idea to have people bring extra clothes, bathing suits, or towels if they want. In our part of the country, the temperature is often eighty-five or ninety degrees on May Day, so we don't mind getting wet! (Green George is a good game to play at Litha and Lammas, too.)

Recipes

When planning a festival, we try to keep everything in theme as best we can. Before, during, and after the ritual, we try to serve food that fits the theme. For example, baked apples, apple pie, pumpkin pie, and mince pie all go well with Samhain and Yule; we often have soup or stew for the main course with fresh baked bread. Decorated eggs and fresh spring fruit add a lot to Imbolg and Ostara. In summer rituals like Beltane, Litha, and Lammas, we tend to have cold sideboards of fresh fruit and vegetables and light, summer sausage. Whenever possible, we try to use traditional recipes. You can find recipes in "ethnic" cookbooks, often along with any history or stories behind them. Here are a few of our favorites.

Wassail (Yule)

6 cups apple cider or juice
1 stick cinnamon
¼ cup honey
3 tablespoons lemon juice
1 32 oz. can pineapple juice
¼ teaspoon grated lemon peel

Heat cider and cinnamon stick to boiling. Reduce heat, cover, and simmer five minutes. Add remaining ingredients and stir. Can be served hot or cold. Serves 12–15.

Mulled Cider (Samhain)

6–8 cloves
1–2 sticks cinnamon
Grated rind of one orange
$^1\!/_2$ cup water
1 32 oz. bottle of apple cider or juice

Put water, spices, and orange rind in a small covered saucepan; heat until boiling. Remove from heat and let stand five minutes, or until the water turns dark from the cinnamon. Place in large pot and add the cider. Heat slowly, over low to medium heat, until heated through. Serve hot. If desired, add a cup of dark, sweet wine, such as a claret, with the cider.

Dark/Irish Oatmeal Cookies (Beltane)

Start with your favorite oatmeal cookie recipe. Substitute molasses for the white sugar, and add two tablespoons of cinnamon and one-half teaspoon of cloves. You may have to add extra flour to get the right consistency.

Crescent Cookies (Lammas)

1 cup butter, softened
2 teaspoons vanilla or almond extract
8 tablespoons powdered confectioners' sugar
2 cups flour
2 cups chopped pecans
extra confectioners' sugar

Preheat oven to 275 degrees. Cream butter and vanilla. Add sugar and beat well. Blend in flour; then stir in nuts with a wooden spoon. Dough will be stiff. Pinch off pieces of dough and shape into crescents. Place on ungreased cookie sheets, and bake about thirty minutes or until light brown. Sprinkle with or roll in the extra confectioners' sugar while warm. Makes 6 dozen.

Gods and Goddesses

The following list gives the basic information about the deities referred to in the text. The information is by no means complete, but it represents the aspects and attributes of the deities that are most important to our purposes. The pronunciation that follows the name is the most common, usually the anglicized or modern pronunciation. When possible, we have placed the meaning of the deity's name in quotation marks following the name itself.

Goddesses

Arianrhod *(ah-ree-AN-hrod)*, "Silver Wheel" — Welsh
The Mother aspect of the Goddess in Wales, Arianrhod is the mother of Lleu Llaw Gyfles and is called the "High Fruitful Mother." She is also a goddess of death and reincarnation; in her palace, Caer *(Kair)* Arianrhod (the Aurora Borealis), she keeps the spirits of the dead until it is time for them to reincarnate. She is also a goddess of the full moon.

Astarte *(as-TAR-tay)* — Canaanite
Often considered a daughter of the Egyptian Ra even though she is Canaanite, Astarte is similar to Ishtar. She was considered a goddess of fertility, and her title was "Queen of the Heavens." She also had a destroying aspect, and like Kali created, destroyed, and created anew.

Blodeuwedd *(BLOH-dew-weth)*, "Flower Face" — Welsh
She was created out of flowers by Gwydion as a wife for Lleu; after she betrayed Lleu, Gwydion turned her into an owl, which became her

bird. She was a Maiden, spring goddess who had connections with the Moon and the lunar mysteries.

Bridget, "Fiery Arrow," or possibly "Power"—Celtic
Most popular in Ireland and Scotland, Bridget was also known in Britain, Gaul, and various other places on the European continent. She was also called Bridget, Brighid, Brigit, Bri'id, Bride, Brigan, Ffraid, and Brigantia. In Ireland she was the daughter of the Dagda and a Goddess of inspiration, poetry, smithcraft, and healing. She is a threefold Goddess and is sometimes portrayed as three sisters all named Bridget. She was adopted by the early Christians both as St. Bridget and as St. Bride; her festival is Imbolg or Candlemas.

Cailleach Beine Bric *(KAY-lee-ahch bayn brik)*—Scots
A Crone aspect of the Goddess, Cailleach is seen as an old woman. She is also called the "Veiled One," and she is considered the spirit of Samhain. Scotland's original name of Caledonia was taken from her name.

Cerridwen *(KAYR-id-wen* or *kayr-RID-u-wen),* "White Grain"—Welsh
Cerridwen was also called Hen Wen or "Old White One" and she was called the "White Sow." She is a goddess of inspiration, the moon, death, and the grain. She is the keeper of the Cauldron of Inspiration, which bestows great knowledge on whoever drinks from it. She is a shapeshifter and the mother of Taliesin.

Danu *(DAH-nu)*—Irish
Also called Dana, Danu is the Mother Goddess of Ireland. It is from her that the Tuatha de Danaan ("people of Danu") take their name. She is connected to the Morrigan in her form of Danu-Ana or Anu.

Diana—Roman
The Roman version of the Greek Artemis, Diana's titles are Goddess of the Moon, Virgin Huntress, and Lady of the Wild Creatures. She is the goddess of the woods and mountains. Probably because of her association with the moon, Diana later became a goddess of magic and witch-

craft. She is the mother of Aradia (Queen of Witches) in the Tuscan witch legends.

Eos — Greek
Goddess of the Dawn and Mother of the Winds, Eos was called "Rosy Fingered Dawn" by Homer. She is the sister of Helios (the sun) and Selene (the moon), and she comes either in a chariot or riding on Pegasus as she brings the dawn.

Eostre *(E-os-ter)* — Saxon
Easter evolved from Eostre's original spring festival. Some sources say she is a goddess of fertility and sacrifice with connections to Astarte and Ishtar. Linguistically, however, her name is derived from the same root as the Old English *ēast*, or "east." She is most likely a goddess of the spring, dawn, and rebirth, which would explain her connections to fertility.

Frigg, "Lady" — Norse
Wife to Odin and mother of Balder, Frigg possessed many magical abilities. As a goddess of fertility, Frigg is considered to have been the same as Freya (Norse goddess of sexual love and keeper of the souls of slain heroes). The two eventually split into separate deities. She is a goddess of the moon and of witches, and her animals are the cat and the falcon.

Gaia *(GĪ-ah)*, "Earth" — Greek
Gaia (also *Gaea* and *Gē*) is called "Mother of the Gods" by Homer; she was the first deity to come from the original chaos. She is the Earth Mother and watched over marriages. The Oracle of Delphi was originally hers.

Hecate *(HEK-ah-tay* or *hek-AH-tay)* — Greek
Originally a Thracian deity, Hecate became very popular in Greece as a goddess of the moon, wisdom, enchantment, and crossroads. She is a threefold goddess, and statues of her looking in three directions were set up to avert evil coming from any side. She also granted victory, protected children, and ruled wandering ghosts.

Inanna *(ee-NAH-nah)* — Sumerian
Daughter of the god Enki, Inanna rules love, weaving, prophesy, the earth, and the heavens. Her title is the "Lady of Heaven," and she was also Goddess of Sovereignty. Her lover was Dumuzi.

Ishtar — Assyro-Babylonian
She was the Great Goddess who appeared as the planet Venus in the heavens. A mother goddess, she ruled many things including the earth, love, the moon, fertility, and marriage. She was also considered the Light of the World. Her temples were watched by Harlot-Priestesses who allowed men access to the Queen of Heaven through "compassionate prostitution."[1]

Kali, "Black" — Hindu
Kali is the Great Destroyer and also a great creative power; she is depicted wearing a necklace of skulls — each of which represents a letter in the Sanskrit alphabet — dancing on a corpse. She is also called "Kali Ma" or the "Black Mother." She is the dark side of the feminine power (Shakti) who clears the way for new growth.

Kore *(kor or KOR-eh)*, "Maiden" — Greek
The name for Persephone before she descended to the Underworld.

Modron, "Mother" — Welsh
Modron is the Great Mother to the Great Son, Mabon. Her son was stolen from her when he was only three days old. The name Modron is used around the British Isles to describe any number of Mother Goddesses.

Morrigan — Irish
Also called "Great Queen" and "Queen of Ghosts," the Morrigan is a war goddess. A triple-aspected deity, she can take the form of a raven, an old hag, or a beautiful young woman.

---

[1] Barbara G. Walker, *The Woman's Encyclopedia of Myths and Secrets* (San Francisco: Harper and Row, 1983), p. 450.

Persephone *(per-SEPH-oh-neh/nay)* — Greek
Persephone in her pre-Classical phase was Queen of the Underworld much like Hecate; later she became a seed goddess and the daughter of Demeter. Her symbol was the pomegranate and the willow was sacred to her. As the daughter of Demeter she was abducted by Hades, King of the Underworld, to be his wife. Until she was returned to her mother, the world was barren and fruitless. Now she spends half the year on Earth and half in the Underworld; when Persephone returns to Earth each year, she brings the spring with her.

Rhiannon *(hree-AN-on)*, "Great Queen" — Welsh
Rhiannon is a horse goddess, the Welsh equivalent of the Continental Celtic goddess, Epona. Rhiannon is an Otherworld goddess who was married first to Pwyll and then to Manawydan; she is connected to the Moon and rules fertility.

Tailltiu *(TAYL-tyu)* — Irish
Tailltiu was the foster mother of Lugh, and the Tailtean Games held at his festival of Lughnasadh were named after her. She is considered an Earth Goddess.

Gods

Adonis, "Lord" — Greek
Adonis was the lover of Aphrodite; when he was killed by a boar, roses (or anemones) sprung from his blood. Like Persephone, Adonis spent half the year on Earth and half in the Underworld.

Anubis *(ah-NU-bis)* — Egyptian
The son of Osiris and Nephthys, jackal-headed Anubis is the Egyptian god of funeral rites and embalming. He guided the soul to the Underworld and then weighed the heart against the feather of truth. He was considered protector of the dead.

Apollo — Greco-Roman
To the Greeks, Apollo was a god of youth, light, music, poetry, fine art, philosophy, and truth. He was brother to Artemis, and both

Apollo and Artemis were called upon to avenge injustice. The laurel tree was sacred to him, and he is often represented holding a bow or a lyre. In addition, the Romans considered him a Sun God.

Attis — Phrygian
Beloved of the goddess Cybele, Attis is a sacrificial vegetation deity. His myth parallels that of Adonis, with violets blooming from his blood.

Balder — Teutonic
The son of Odin and Frigg, Balder was a god of light, purity, and beauty, who represented everything wholesome and good. He was slain by Loki, but at the end of the world he will return to rule a new Earth.

Beli — Welsh
Father of Arianrhod and husband to Don, Beli is a "father" type deity similar to Belinus.

Belinus, "Shining" — Continental Celtic
Belinus (or Belenos) is a solar or fire deity whom the Romans equated with Apollo; he rules over crops and cattle and was called on for healing. The Celtic festival of Beltane is named for him.

Cernunnos *(KER-nu-nos* or *ker-NU-nos)*, "Horned One" — Continental Celtic
Cernunnos is "Lord of the Animals" and "Keeper of the Gates of Life and Death." A stag god, he is depicted sitting cross-legged holding a torque and a ram-headed serpent. Originally a hunting god, Cernunnos later took on attributes of fertility and prosperity.

Dumuzi *(du-MU-zi)* — Sumerian
The lover of Inanna, Dumuzi is equated with Tammuz and has the double role of being a vegetation god and a god of the Underworld. He was known as "the shepherd" and "Lord of the Sheepfolds." The sur-

viving fragments of the myth of Inanna and Dumuzi break off before the end of the story, so we do not know if Dumuzi is brought back from the Underworld.

Faunus — Roman
Faunus is a nature deity who protected the forests and fields. He was a patron of shepherds and their flocks.

Ganesha *(GAH-nesh-ah* or *gah-NAY-shah)* — Hindu
The most popular god of the Hindu Pantheon, Ganesha is a deity of good fortune, wisdom, and literature. He is the god invoked before a new venture, for he can open or close the door of success. The son of Parvati, he is depicted with the head of an elephant.

Green Man — British Isles
The Green Man is found all over Britain and Europe as the Foliate Mask: a representation of a human face made up of twining vegetation and greenery, often with leafy branches emerging from the mouth. He is the spirit of the forest and the trees, a god of the woodlands. He appears at May Day as "Green George" or "Jack-in-the-Green."

Gwydion *(GWI-dee-on)* — Welsh
A bard, magician, and shapeshifter, Gwydion is invoked in matters of healing and magic. He tricked Arianrhod into giving Lleu a name and arms. He created Blodeuwedd as a wife for Lleu and later turned her into an owl. He is the son of Beli and Don, and his symbol is the white horse.

Gwynn ap Nudd *(gwin ahp nuth)* — Welsh
Gwynn is god of the Underworld and leads a Wild Hunt. His worship was centered at Glastonbury Tor; legend has it that this was his home.

Hades *(HAY-dees)* — Greek
God of the Underworld, Hades stole Persephone away from Demeter. He is also a god of prosperity who guards the great riches of the Earth.

Helios *(HEE-lee-os)* — Greek
Helios is a Sun God, brother to Eos. From his sun chariot, Helios sees everything on earth and in heaven.

Herne *(hern)* — English
A blend of the Saxon Woden and the Celtic Cernunnos, Herne shares the attributes of both. He is a forest and hunting deity and leads the Wild Hunt during the winter months. The oak is his sacred tree and the stag, his animal. He is said to appear in Windsor Park at times of national distress or when one of the monarchs of Britain is about to die.

Lleu Llaw Gyffes *(hlu hlaw gifs)*, "Bright One with a Skillful Hand" — Welsh
Son of Arianrhod, Lleu is connected with the sun, art, smiths, bards, and war. He is the Welsh form of Lugh, and the Romans equated him with Mercury. Lammas is his festival, and the eagle is his symbol.

Mabon *(MAH-bon)*, "Son" — Welsh
Also called the "Great Prisoner," Mabon is the Celtic divine child. He was stolen as a child and imprisoned; he was later freed by Arthur. Mabon is connected with prophecy, music, harmony, and freedom.

Manawydan *(man-a-WID-an)* — Welsh
Son of Llyr, Manawydan was the second husband of Rhiannon. He is the Welsh version of Manannan and is a god of the sea, storms, and fertility.

Manannan *(mah-NAN-an)* — Irish
Son of Ler, Manannan is a god of the sea and of storms; the lightning bolt was his sword. He is a chieftain god and a shapeshifter. His boat needed no sails or oars, propelled only by his will. He was also skilled at divination and possessed magical animals.

Maponus *(mah-POH-nus)* — Romano-British
Latin name for Mabon.

Mithras *(MITH-ras)* — Persian
A Persian deity of light and the sun, Mithras was so well-liked by the Roman military that his worship spread even into the British Isles. There is a shrine to Mithras in the middle of London.

Nuada *(nu-AH-dah)* — Irish
King of the Tuatha de Danaan, Nuada was a god of healing and was connected to the idea of sacred kingship; he gave up his place as leader when he lost his hand in battle. The lost hand was replaced with a silver one, earning him the title "Silver Hand." He has connections with water and has been compared to Neptune.

Osiris *(oh-SĪ-ris*, or *o-SIR-is)*, "Seat of the Eye" — Egyptian
Osiris is a vegetation and fertility god as well as the Lord of the Underworld. He was killed by his brother Set and restored to life by his wife, Isis. His death and rebirth represent the planting ("burial") of the seed and its eventual sprouting ("rebirth").

Pan — Greek
A woodland deity and a patron of shepherds and their flocks, Pan is credited with inventing the reed pipe ("Pan pipe"). The Romans equated him with Faunus.

Pelles *(PEL-les)* — British
One of the names of the Fisher King in the Grail Legends; King Pelles was wounded, and the land was blighted and barren until he was healed by the Holy Grail. The Sacred King whose health is directly tied to the fertility of the land is the Celtic version of the Dying and Rising God.

Robin, "Shining" — British
Robin or Robin Hood is connected to the May Day festivities and has long been associated with the Wiccan faith — "Robin" is a synonym for the High Priest. Robin is also connected to the spirit of the greenwood and the forests.

Taliesin *(tal-ee-AY-sin)*, "Radiant Brow" — Welsh
Son of Cerridwen, Taliesin is the patron of mortal bards and rules over poetry, music, and knowledge. (The mythic Taliesin should not be confused with the historic Taliesin, a Welsh bard who lived in the sixth century.)

Tammuz *(TAH-muz)* — Assyro-Babylonian
The best-known dying and rising vegetation deity, Tammuz was the beloved of Ishtar. She traveled to the Underworld and brought him back to life, but Tammuz must return to the Underworld every winter.

Woden *(WOH-den)* — Saxon
Woden is the Saxon form of Odin, although he isn't quite as much of a trickster figure as Odin. Woden is a deity of death, battle, and poetic inspiration; he also leads the Wild Hunt. He is invoked in matters dealing with magic, poetry, war, and the Underworld.

Research Tips and Suggested Reading

In the "How to Write a Ritual" section of this book, we recommended that you start with research. Where? How? Here are a few hints on the easiest way to do research:

1) Start with our bibliography.
We recommend that you start with the bibliography in the back of this book for a few reasons. First, it's in your hands right now and you don't have to go anywhere. Second, most of the books in our bibliography are new, or at least still in print, and should be available in any good library or bookstore. Third, we have arranged our bibliography by subject to make it easier to find what you're looking for. Interested in reading more about ritual? See the "Ritual" heading. Folk customs? See "Folk Customs/Ancient Religions." Easy. We have also tried to indicate what subject heading these books would be found under in a library; with these subject headings you can even find other books that we didn't use. Books that cover more than one subject are listed under each one, and books we recommend are marked with an asterisk. Two asterisks means the book is exceptional and highly recommended.

So start with the books we used and see if they have anything that interests you. Anytime you find a book you like, check *its* bibliography, and so on. Books that show up over and over again in bibliographies are likely to be worth looking at.

2) Check footnotes and endnotes.
If we quote a particular thing that you liked, check our footnotes and

see where we got it. Ditto for any other book. Kind authors will give you complete information about the sources they quote from, so you can find the original if you want to.

3) Remember your purpose.
There is just as much bad research as good in any field, but the field of myth and folklore is especially vulnerable to poor scholarship. Authors have to try to reconstruct the beliefs and practices of people who lived centuries ago from a few stray works of architecture and fragments of verse. It is easy to mistranslate and misinterpret, to apply all the attributes of one deity to another because of a coincidental similarity in name or myth. Also, many authors will start their research with a particular theory or purpose in mind; sometimes, any information that contradicts their theory is conveniently ignored.

Now, just because an author's scholarship isn't very good doesn't mean that the book won't be any good when researching for a ritual. Remember, your purpose in researching isn't to get a completely accurate idea of what the holiday is and how it was celebrated; your purpose is to get ideas. If a book inspires you or gives you an idea for your ritual, by all means use it, even if you know that the author is completely wrong. It doesn't matter. It's the inspiration that you're after, not the information. Trying to have a completely accurate understanding of the holiday is not as important as having a good ritual.

Selected Reading by Subject

The following books appear in the general bibliography, but we are listing them again so you can explore various subjects. We have recommended some titles more than others; * after the title means we really liked the book and ** means that the title is highly recommended.

FOLK CUSTOMS/ANCIENT RELIGIONS

Anderson, William. *Green Man.***

Athanassakis, Apostolos. *The Homeric Hymns.**

Athanassakis, Apostolos. *The Orphic Hymns.**

Bord, Janet and Colin. *Earth Rites.***

Bord, Janet and Colin. *Sacred Waters.***

Burkert, Walter. *Greek Religion.*

Campanelli, Pauline. *Wheel of the Year.***

Chambers, E.K. *The English Folk Play.**

Conway, D.J. *Celtic Magic.**

Conway, D.J. *Norse Magic.**

Cosman, Madeleine Pelner. *Medieval Holidays and Festivals.***

Cunningham, Scott. *Cunningham's Encyclopedia of Magical Herbs.***

Cunningham, Scott. *Magical Herbalism.***

Eliade, Mircea. *Cosmos and History.***

Eliade, Mircea. *The Sacred and the Profane.***

Frazer, Sir James George. *The Golden Bough.**

Gantz, Jeffrey. *Early Irish Myths and Sagas.***

Gardner, Gerald B. *The Meaning of Witchcraft.**

Gimbutas, Marija. *The Language of the Goddess.***

Glass-Koentop, Pattalee. *Year of Moons, Season of Trees.***

Graves, Robert. *The Greek Myths (in two volumes).***

Graves, Robert. *The White Goddess.**

Grimes, Ronald L. *Research in Ritual Studies.**

Harvey, Sir Paul. *Oxford Companion to Classical Literature.***

Hooke, S. H. *Middle Eastern Mythology.***

Jung, Emma and M. L. von Franz. *The Grail Legend.*

Kightly, Charles. *The Perpetual Almanac of Folklore.**

Lehane, Brendan. *The Book of Christmas.***

Leland, Charles. *Aradia: The Gospel of the Witches.***

MacCana, Proinsias. *Celtic Mythology.**
Markale, Jean. *Women of the Celts.***
Matthews, Caitlin. *Elements of the Celtic Tradition.***
Michell, John. *The Earth Spirit.*
Murray, Liz and Colin. *The Celtic Tree Oracle.***
O'Driscoll, Robert (ed.). *Celtic Consciousness.***
Phillis, Guy. *Brigantia.***
Rees, Alwyn and Brinley. *Celtic Heritage.***
Sharkey, John. *Celtic Mysteries.**
Stewart, Bob. *Pagan Imagery in English Folksong.**
Toulson, Shirley. *Winter Solstice.***
Turner, Victor Witter. *Celebration.***
Turner, Victor Witter. *The Ritual Process.***
Weston, Jesse. *From Ritual to Romance.*
Weston, Jesse. *The Quest of the Holy Grail.*

HERBALISM
Buckland, Raymond. *Buckland's Complete Book of Witchcraft.**
Cunningham, Scott. *Cunningham's Encyclopedia of Magical Herbs.***
Cunningham, Scott. *Magical Herbalism.***

LITERARY WORKS/STUDIES
Athanassakis, Apostolos. *The Homeric Hymns.**
Athanassakis, Apostolos. *The Orphic Hymns.**
Gantz, Jeffrey. *Early Irish Myths and Sagas.***
Gantz, Jeffrey (trans.). *The Mabinogion.**
Graves, Robert. *The White Goddess.**
Guest, Lady Charlotte (trans.). *The Mabinogion.**
Harvey, Sir Paul. *Oxford Companion to Classical Literature.***
Jackson, Kenneth Hurlstone. *A Celtic Miscellany.*
Stewart, Bob. *Pagan Imagery in English Folksong.**

MYTH-LEGEND
Anderson, William. *Green Man.***
Aswynn, Freya. *Leaves of Yggdrasil.***
Athanassakis, Apostolos. *The Homeric Hymns.**
Athanassakis, Apostolos. *The Orphic Hymns.**
Bord, Janet and Colin. *Earth Rites.***

Bord, Janet and Colin. *Sacred Waters.***
Bullfinch, Thomas. *Mythology.*
Conway, D.J. *Celtic Magic.**
Conway, D.J. *Norse Magic.**
Eliade, Mircea. *Cosmos and History.***
Eliade, Mircea. *The Sacred and the Profane.***
Farrar, Janet and Stewart. *The Witches' God.***
Farrar, Janet and Stewart. *The Witches' Goddess.***
Gantz, Jeffrey. *Early Irish Myths and Sagas.***
Gantz, Jeffrey (trans.). *The Mabinogion.**
Gardner, Gerald B. *The Meaning of Witchcraft.**
Glass-Koentop, Pattalee. *Year of Moons, Season of Trees.***
Grant, Michael. *Myths of the Greeks and Romans.*
Graves, Robert. *The Greek Myths (in two volumes).***
Graves, Robert. *The White Goddess.**
Grimal, Pierre (editor). *Larousse World Mythology.*
Guest, Lady Charlotte (trans.). *The Mabinogion.**
Harvey, Sir Paul. *Oxford Companion to Classical Literature.***
Hooke, S. H. *Middle Eastern Mythology.***
Jung, Emma and M. L. von Franz. *The Grail Legend.*
Kirk, G. S. *Myth.*
Long, Charles H. *Alpha: Myths of Creation.**
MacCana, Proinsias. *Celtic Mythology.**
MacKenzie, Donald. *German Myths and Legends.*
Mann, Nicholas. *Keltic Power Symbols.***
Markale, Jean. *Women of the Celts.***
Matthews, Caitlin. *Elements of the Celtic Tradition.***
Matthews, Caitlin. *Mabon & the Mysteries of Britain.**
McGarry, Mary. *Great Folk Tales of Old Ireland.*
Michell, John. *The Earth Spirit.*
Monaghan, Patricia. *The Book of Goddesses and Heroines.**
Murray, Liz and Colin. *The Celtic Tree Oracle.***
Murray, Margaret. *The God of the Witches.**
O'Driscoll, Robert (ed.). *Celtic Consciousness.***
Phillis, Guy. *Brigantia.***
Rees, Alwyn and Brinley. *Celtic Heritage.***
Robinson, Herbert and Knox Wilson. *Myths of All Nations.*

Sharkey, John. *Celtic Mysteries.**
Sjoestedt, Marie-Louise. *Gods and Heroes of the Celts.***
Starhawk. *The Spiral Dance.***
Stewart, Bob. *Pagan Imagery in English Folksong.**
Stewart, R. J. *Celtic Gods, Celtic Goddesses.***
Toulson, Shirley. *Winter Solstice.***
Walter, Barbara G. *The Woman's Encyclopedia of Myths and Secrets.***
Weston, Jesse. *From Ritual to Romance.*
Weston, Jesse. *The Quest of the Holy Grail.*
Williamson, John. *The Oak King, the Holly King & the Unicorn.**

RITUAL

Beck, Renee and Sydney Barbara Metrick. *The Art of Ritual.*
Buckland, Raymond. *Buckland's Complete Book of Witchcraft.**
Buckland, Raymond. *The Tree.**
Burkert, Walter. *Greek Religion.*
Christ, Carol & Judith Plaskow (ed.). *Womanspirit Rising.**
Eliade, Mircea. *Cosmos and History.***
Eliade, Mircea. *The Sacred and the Profane.***
Fitch, Ed. *Magical Rites from the Crystal Well.*
Glass-Koentop, Pattalee. *Year of Moons, Season of Trees.***
Grimes, Ronald L. *Research in Ritual Studies.**
Harvey, Sir Paul. *Oxford Companion to Classical Literature.***
Slater, Herman (ed.). *A Book of Pagan Rituals.**
Starhawk. *The Spiral Dance.***
Turner, Victor Witter. *Celebration: Studies in Festivals & Rituals.***
Turner, Victor Witter. *The Ritual Process.***
Weinstein, Marion. *Earth Magic.***
Weston, Jesse. *From Ritual to Romance.*

SEASONAL HOLIDAYS

Adler, Margot. *Drawing Down the Moon.***
Beck, Renee and Barbara Metrick. *The Art of Ritual.*
Bord, Janet and Colin. *Earth Rites.***
Buckland, Raymond. *Buckland's Complete Book of Witchcraft.**
Buckland, Raymond. *The Tree.**
Burkert, Walter. *Greek Religion.*
Campanelli, Pauline. *Wheel of the Year.***
Chambers, E.K. *The English Folk Play.**

Conway, D.J. *Celtic Magic.**
Cosman, Madeleine Pelner. *Medieval Holidays and Festivals.***
Farrar, Janet and Stewart. *Eight Sabbats for Witches.***
Frazer, Sir James George. *The Golden Bough.**
Glass-Koentop, Pattalee. *Year of Moons, Season of Trees.***
Harvey, Sir Paul. *Oxford Companion to Classical Literature.***
Kightly, Charles. *The Perpetual Almanac of Folklore.**
Lehane, Brendan. *The Book of Christmas.***
Matthews, Caitlin. *Elements of the Celtic Tradition.***
Murray, Liz and Colin. *The Celtic Tree Oracle.***
Rees, Alwyn and Brinley. *Celtic Heritage.***
Starhawk. *The Spiral Dance.***
Toulson, Shirley. *Winter Solstice.***
Weinstein, Marion. *Earth Magic.***

WICCA

Adler, Margot. *Drawing Down the Moon.***
Buckland, Raymond. *Buckland's Complete Book of Witchcraft.**
Buckland, Raymond. *The Tree.**
Campanelli, Pauline. *Wheel of the Year.***
Christ, Carol & Judith Plaskow (ed.). *Womanspirit Rising.**
Crowther, Patricia. *Lid off the Cauldron.***
Farrar, Janet and Stewart. *Eight Sabbats for Witches.***
Fitch, Ed. *Magical Rites from the Crystal Well.*
Gardner, Gerald B. *Meaning of Witchcraft.**
Gardner, Gerald B. *Witchcraft Today.**
Glass-Koentop, Pattalee. *Year of Moons, Season of Trees.***
Leland, Charles. *Aradia: The Gospel of the Witches.***
Melton, J. Gordon. *Magic, Witchcraft, and Paganism.**
Murray, Margaret. *The God of the Witches.**
Ryall, Rhiannon. *West Country Wicca.***
Slater, Herman (ed.). *A Book of Pagan Rituals.*
Starhawk. *The Spiral Dance.***
Valiente, Doreen. *An ABC of Witchcraft Past & Present.***
Valiente, Doreen. *The Rebirth of Witchcraft.***
Valiente, Doreen. *Witchcraft for Tomorrow.***
Valiente, Doreen. *Witchcraft: A Tradition Renewed.***
Weinstein, Marion. *Earth Magic.***

Bibliography

Adler, Margot. *Drawing Down the Moon: Witches, Druids, Goddess-Worshippers and Other Pagans in America Today.* Boston: Beacon Press, 1990.

Anderson, William. *Green Man: The Archetype of Our Oneness with the Earth.* London: HarperCollins, 1990.

Aswynn, Freya. *Leaves of Yggdrasil.* St. Paul, MN: Llewellyn, 1990.

Athanassakis, Apostolos. *The Homeric Hymns.* Baltimore: Johns Hopkins University Press, 1978.

————. *The Orphic Hymns: Text, Translation and Notes.* Atlanta, GA: Scholar's Press, 1988.

Beck, Renee and Sydney Barbara Metrick. *The Art of Ritual.* Berkeley, CA: Celestial Arts, 1990.

Bord, Janet and Colin. *Earth Rites.* London: Book Club Associates, 1982.

————. *Sacred Waters: Holy Wells and Water Lore in Britain and Ireland.* London: Granada, 1985.

Buckland, Raymond. *Buckland's Complete Book of Witchcraft.* St. Paul, MN: Llewellyn, 1986.

————. *The Tree: Complete Book of Saxon Witchcraft.* York Beach, ME: Samuel Weiser, 1974.

Bullfinch, Thomas. *Mythology.* New York: Dell, 1959.

Burkert, Walter. *Greek Religion*, trans. John Raffan. Cambridge, MA: Harvard University Press, 1985.

Campanelli, Pauline. *Wheel of the Year: Living the Magickal Life.* St. Paul, MN: Llewellyn, 1989.

Cavendish, Richard, ed. *Man, Myth, and Magic: The Illustrated Encyclo-*

pedia of Mythology, Religion and the Unknown. 24 Vols. New York: Marshall Cavendish, 1983.

Chambers, E.K. *The English Folk Play.* Oxford: Clarendon Press, 1933. Reprint. Blythebourne Sta., Brooklyn, NY: Haskell, 1966.

Christ, Carol & Judith Plaskow, ed. *Womanspirit Rising: A Reader in Religion.* San Francisco: HarperCollins, 1979.

Conway, Deanna J. *Celtic Magic.* St. Paul, MN: Llewellyn, 1990.

———. *Norse Magic.* St. Paul, MN: Llewellyn, 1990.

Cosman, Madeleine Pelner. *Medieval Holidays and Festivals: A Calendar of Celebrations.* New York: Charles Scribner's Sons, 1981.

Crowther, Patricia. *Lid Off the Cauldron.* York Beach, ME: Samuel Weiser, 1989.

Cunningham, Scott. *Cunningham's Encyclopedia of Crystal, Gem, and Metal Magic.* St. Paul, MN: Llewellyn, 1987.

———. *Cunningham's Encyclopedia of Magical Herbs.* St. Paul, MN: Llewellyn, 1985.

———. *Magical Herbalism: The Secret Craft of the Wise.* St. Paul, MN: Llewellyn, 1983.

Eliade, Mircea. *Cosmos and History.* New York: Harper Torchbooks, 1959.

———. *The Sacred and the Profane: The Nature of Religion.* Magnolia, MA: Peter Smith, 1983.

Farrar, Janet and Stewart. *Eight Sabbats for Witches: And Rites for Birth, Marriage and Death.* Custer, WA: Phoenix, 1981.

———. *The Witches' God: Lord of the Dance.* Custer, WA: Phoenix, 1989.

———. *The Witches' Goddess.* Custer, WA: Phoenix, 1987.

Fitch, Ed. *Magical Rites from the Crystal Well.* St. Paul, MN: Llewellyn, 1984.

Frazer, Sir James George. *The Golden Bough.* New York: Macmillan, 1922.

Gantz, Jeffrey. *Early Irish Myths and Sagas.* London: Penguin Books, 1981.

Gantz, Jeffrey (trans.). *The Mabinogion.* London: Penguin Books, 1976.

Gardner, Gerald B. *Meaning of Witchcraft.* New York: Magickal Childe, 1982.

―――. *Witchcraft Today.* New York: Magickal Childe, 1982.

Gimbutas, Marija. *The Language of the Goddess: Unearthing the Hidden Symbols of Western Civilization.* San Francisco: HarperCollins, 1991.

Glass-Koentop, Pattalee. *Year of Moons, Season of Trees: Mysteries and Rites of Celtic Tree Magic.* St. Paul, MN: Llewellyn, 1991.

Grant, Michael. *Myths of the Greeks and Romans.* New York: Mentor Books, 1962.

Graves, Robert. *The Greek Myths.* 2 Vols. London: Penguin Books, 1986.

―――. *The White Goddess: A Historical Grammar of Poetic Myth.* New York: Farrar, Strauss, & Giroux, 1966.

Grimal, Pierre (editor). *Larousse Encyclopedia of World Mythology.* New York: Excalibur Books, 1981.

Grimes, Ronald L. *Research in Ritual Studies: A Programmatic Essay and Bibliography.* Metuchen, NJ: Scarecrow, 1985.

Guest, Lady Charlotte (trans.). *The Mabinogion.* Chicago: Academy Chicago, 1978 (facsimile of the 1871 edition).

Gundarsson, Kveldulf. *Teutonic Magic: The Magical and Spiritual Practices of the Germanic Peoples.* St. Paul, MN: Llewellyn, 1990.

Harvey, Sir Paul. *The Oxford Companion to Classical Literature.* 1937. Reprint. Oxford: Oxford University Press, 1986.

Hooke, S. H. *Middle Eastern Mythology.* London: Penguin Books, 1963.

Jackson, Kenneth Hurlstone. *A Celtic Miscellany.* New York: Dorset Press, 1951.

Jung, Emma and M. L. von Franz. *The Grail Legend.* Boston: Sigo, 1986.

Kightly, Charles. *The Perpetual Almanac of Folklore.* London: Thames & Hudson, 1987.

Kirk, G. S. *Myth: Its Meaning and Functions in Ancient and Other Cultures.* Berkeley, CA: University of California Press, 1970.

Lehane, Brendan. *The Book of Christmas.* Chicago: Time-Life, 1986.

Leland, Charles. *Aradia: Gospel of the Witches.* Custer, WA: Phoenix, 1989.

Long, Charles H. *Alpha: The Myths of Creation.* Chicago: Scholar's Press, 1963.

MacCana, Proinsias. *Celtic Mythology.* New York: Peter Bedrick, 1991; and Feltham, England: Newnes Books, 1968.

MacKenzie, Donald. *German Myths and Legends.* New York: Avenal Books, 1985.

Mann, Nicholas. *Keltic Power Symbols.* Glastonbury, England: Triskele, 1987.

Markale, Jean. *Women of the Celts.* Rochester, VT: Inner Traditions International, 1986.

Matthews, Caitlin. *Elements of the Celtic Tradition.* Shaftesbury, England: Element Books, 1989.

————. *Mabon & the Mysteries of Britain.* London: Arkana, Penguin, 1987.

McGarry, Mary. *Great Folk Tales of Old Ireland.* New York: Bell Publishing Company, 1952.

Melton, J. Gordon. *Magic, Witchcraft, and Paganism in America.* New York: Gorland Publishing, 1982.

Michell, John. *The Earth Spirit: Its Ways, Shrines, & Mysteries.* New York: Thames & Hudson, 1989.

Monaghan, Patricia. *The Book of Goddesses and Heroines.* St. Paul, MN: Llewellyn, 1990.

Murray, Liz and Colin. *The Celtic Tree Oracle.* New York: St. Martin's Press, 1988.

Murray, Margaret. *The God of the Witches.* Oxford: Oxford University Press, 1970.

O'Driscoll, Robert (ed.). *The Celtic Consciousness.* New York: George Braziller, 1982.

Phillis, Guy. *Brigantia.* London: Routledge & Kegan Paul, 1976.

Rees, Alwyn and Brinley. *Celtic Heritage: Ancient Tradition in Ireland & Wales.* New York: Thames & Hudson, 1989.

Robinson, Herbert and Knox Wilson. *Myths & Legends of All Nations.* Lanam, MO: Littlefield, 1978.

Rothovius, Andrew. "Quarter Days and Cross-Quarter Days." *The Old Farmer's Almanac,* no. 201:1993. Dublin, NH: Yankee Publishing, 1992.

Ryall, Rhiannon. *West Country Wicca.* Custer, WA: Phoenix, 1990.

Sharkey, John. *Celtic Mysteries.* New York: Thames & Hudson, 1987.

Sjoestedt, Marie-Louise. *Gods and Heroes of the Celts.* Berkeley, CA: Turtle Island Foundation, 1982.

Slater, Herman (ed.). *A Book of Pagan Rituals.* York Beach, ME: Samuel Weiser, 1978.

Starhawk. *The Spiral Dance.* San Francisco: HarperCollins, 1989.

Stewart, Bob. *Pagan Imagery in English Folksong.* Atlantic Highlands, NJ: Humanties Press, 1977.

Stewart, R. J. *Celtic Gods, Celtic Goddesses.* London: Blandford, 1990.

Toulson, Shirley. *Winter Solstice.* London: Jill Norman and Hobhouse, 1981.

Turner, Victor Witter. *Celebration: Studies in Festivity & Ritual.* Washington: Smithsonian Institute Press, 1982.

———. *The Ritual Process: Structure and Anti-Structure.* Chicago: Aldine de Gruyter, 1969.

Valiente, Doreen. *An ABC of Witchcraft: Past and Present.* New York: St. Martin's Press, 1973.

———. *Natural Magic.* London: Robert Hale, 1975.

———. *The Rebirth of Witchcraft.* Custer, WA: Phoenix; London: Robert Hale, 1989.

———. *Witchcraft: A Tradition Renewed.* Custer. WA: Phoenix, 1990.

———. *Witchcraft for Tomorrow.* Custer, WA: Phoenix; London: Robert Hale, 1978.

Walker, Barbara G. *The Woman's Encyclopedia of Myths and Secrets.* San Francisco: HarperCollins, 1983.

Weinstein, Marion. *Earth Magic: A Dianic Book of Shadows.* Custer, WA: Phoenix, 1980.

Weston, Jessie. *From Ritual to Romance.* Magnolia, MA: Peter Smith, n.d.

———. *The Quest of the Holy Grail.* New York: Barnes and Noble, 1964.

Williamson, John. *The Oak King, the Holly King & the Unicorn.* New York: HarperCollins, 1986.

Resource List

BOOKS/TAPES/GENERAL MERCHANDISE

Circle
P.O. Box 219
Mt. Horeb, WI 53572
(Circle offers a newsletter, *Circle Network News,* which has many re-
sources available. They sell books, tapes, statues, and jewelry.)

The Gaia Bookstore
1400 Shattuck Avenue at Rose
Berkeley, CA 94709
(The Gaia Bookstore has a wide selection of merchandise including
books, statues, jewelry, tapes, drums, and rattles.)

MUSIC

Ladyslipper, Inc.
P.O. Box 3124-R
Durham, NC 27715
(Ladyslipper deals in women's music of all kinds and is an excellent
source of Goddess-oriented tapes and CD's. Their catalogue is huge and
very well organized into categories so that it's easy to find the right
tape.)

Chivalry Sports
P.O. Box 18904
Tucson, AZ 85731-8904
(They offer the Rose and Nefr Dance Course, a well-researched in-
struction manual for over fifty medieval and renaissance dances. In-
cludes two tapes of live music performed on medieval instruments.
This company is a source for medieval recreationists and is not Pagan
affiliated.)

Spring Hill Music
P.O. Box 800
Boulder, CO 80306
(Source of "From the Goddess" tape by On Wings of Song and Robert
Gass.)

GODDESS/GOD REPRODUCTIONS & STATUES

Star River Productions, Inc.
P.O. Box 6254
North Brunswick, NJ 08902
(Star River offers museum quality Goddess reproductions. Their
statues are some of the best and they cover a wide range of cultures.
They have recently expanded their catalogue to include other Goddess-
oriented merchandise. They are prompt and very pleasant to deal with.)

Grand Adventure
RD6 Box 6198A
Stroudsberg, PA 18360
(Grand Adventure also offers Goddess statues of an unusual nature.
One example of their hard to find goddesses is a Cucuteni figure from
Roumania. The figures are well-made, attractive and quite reasonable
in their prices.)

Church of All Worlds
P.O. Box 1542
Ukiah, CA 95482

(CAW publishes the *Green Egg,* one of the most professional and entertaining of the Pagan magazines. They also sell a growing line of Goddess and God statues and have some very fine jewelry available in sterling and bronze.)

ORIGINAL ART

Trish McCall
P.O. Box 170298
Irving, TX 75017
(All linoleum block prints in *Seasonal Dance* can be ordered from the artist for $25.00 each. To get further information or to order write Trish at the above address.)

Karen Edie
P.O. Box 170298
Irving, TX 75017
(Karen does wonderful paintings in watercolors and oils. She is an excellent source for representations of goddesses or gods that are more obscure and hard to find. She makes beautiful "Icon" style triptychs painted on wood for altars and will work with you to get exactly what you have in mind realized in your painting. Prices vary according to medium and details involved but are very reasonable for the quality of work she does. Most prices will fall in the $25-$100 range.)

Moonheart Pottery
P.O. Box 170298
Irving, TX 75017
(Moonheart Pottery has pottery altar items available that are functional as well as beautiful. Dishes to hold herbs for element offerings, chalices, candleholders and more are produced in high fire stoneware. Special order items are taken on an individual pricing basis.)

HERBS

Years to Your Health
503 E. 2nd Street
Irving, TX 75060
(Years offers a free catalogue and has a great inventory of herbs available. They are friendly and helpful as well as informed on their subject.)

Note: Inclusion in this list of resources does not necessarily denote a Pagan supplier.

Index

About the Authors

Veronica MacLer is a student of myth and folklore who began writing poetry and fiction when she was 15. She has a Bachelor of Arts in English Literature with minors in Latin and Greek from the University of Dallas, and has been teaching English as a second language to adult students for the past five years. She is a Dianic High Priestess and founding member of the Greenwood Path. She is currently in Texas where she lives the pagan and shamanistic way.

Janice Broch has a Bachelor's degree in English with minors in Journalism and Art from North Texas State University. She has been involved with Wicca for twenty years and teaches students in the Wiccan tradition. Broch became a High Priestess in the Dianic tradition in the early 80s and is a founding member of the Greenwood Path. Her love of the arts has led her to create, with her husband, handmade pottery that reflects nature, but in the future she wishes to combine her artistic talents with her writing. She lives in Texas with her husband.